Penguin Handbooks
More Easy Cooking for One or Two

Louise Davies left King's College of Household and Social Science (now King's College, London) with a B.Sc. degree and a conviction that scientists need interpreting. She has therefore combined the study of nutrition with writing, broadcasting, interviewing, lecturing and television appearances. At the Ministry of Food she wrote a monthly magazine, *Food and Nutrition*, for dietitians and home economics teachers. Her first book, *See How to Cook*, was a pioneer amongst picture cookery books. For twelve years she broadcast *Shopping List* twice weekly in the B.B.C *Today* programme, giving advice on shopping and recipes, and combining this and other broadcasts with a busy home life. Now, as head of the Gerontology Nutrition Unit at the Royal Free Hospital School of Medicine, she is conducting research into nutritional needs before and after the age of retirement from work and is actively encouraging practical help for those who shop for one or two, recipients of meals on wheels and residents in homes for elderly people. She gained a Ph.D. with the thesis 'Dietary Survey on a Group of Elderly People', later rewritten as a book, *Three Score Years . . . and Then* (1981). She is the author of *Easy Cooking for One or Two* (Penguin 1972) and *Easy Cooking for Three or More* (Penguin 1975). A new edition of *Easy Cooking for One or Two* was published in 1988. In 1978 she was awarded an International Prize in Modern Nutrition. She has advised on osteoporosis and malnutrition of the elderly for the World Health Organisation and is a member of the International Union of Nutritional Sciences Committee on Geriatric Nutrition. Louise Davies is a widow with two daughters.

Louise Davies

More Easy Cooking for One or Two

ILLUSTRATED BY
Tony Odell

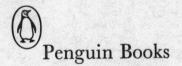
Penguin Books

PENGUIN BOOKS

Published by the Penguin Group
Penguin Books Ltd, 27 Wrights Lane, London W8 5TZ, England
Viking Penguin, a division of Penguin Books USA Inc.
375 Hudson Street, New York, New York 10014, USA
Penguin Books Australia Ltd, Ringwood, Victoria, Australia
Penguin Books Canada Ltd, 2801 John Street, Markham, Ontario, Canada L3R 1B4
Penguin Books (NZ) Ltd, 182–190 Wairau Road, Auckland 10, New Zealand

Penguin Books Ltd, Registered Offices: Harmondsworth, Middlesex, England

First published 1979
10 9 8 7 6

Printed in England by Clays Ltd, St Ives plc
Set in Monotype Baskerville

With gratitude to Miss Kathleen Lockley
and Miss Frances Marston,
my Headmistress and English teacher
at the Brighton and Hove
High School (G.P.D.S.T.)

Contents

Introduction

The enthusiastic reception given to *Easy Cooking for One or Two* has encouraged me to repeat the dose in this companion volume. 'The dose' being my favourite form of *preventive* medicine: nourishing food, easy to prepare.

Every chapter in this book is designed for the differing needs and abilities of the elderly. But it is also for anyone of any age who is cooking in small quantities.

In this book there are two major additions:

1. Some old-fashioned remedies, i.e. the prize-winning recipes from a cookery competition in *Yours*, the newspaper produced by Help the Aged. These old-time favourites were submitted by men and women in their sixties, seventies, eighties and even nineties.

2. A tonic, called 'Cooking for Companionship'. Guaranteed to aid in the prevention of loneliness. The recipes in this chapter are also an effective treatment for the strain (on purse or person) of entertaining.

Acknowledgements

I am indebted to teachers and students of 'Over 60s' and 'Retirement Cookery' classes who have sent in or commented on many of the recipes in this book.

Among home economists who have suggested several recipes or ideas are friends working for the British Farm Produce Council, British Gas, the Canned Food Advisory Service, Danish Agricultural Producers, the Electricity Council, the Flour Advisory Bureau, the Herring Industry Board, the Meat Promotion Executive, the National Dairy Council, the New Zealand Lamb Information Bureau, R.H.M. Foods and Van den Berghs and Jurgens.

Diane Holdsworth and Nancy Sienkiewicz have once again supported me as I sagged during the production of this book.

A special thank you is due to Cynthia Disley, Lecturer in Food Studies, Hounslow Borough College, for giving me tested recipes from her classes and invaluable advice on the first draft.

Chapter 1
Recipes for Non-cooks

This chapter is especially written for the non-cook, that is:

- anybody who has never learned to cook.
- anybody who cannot physically manage the preparation of meals.
- anybody who is just not interested in cooking.
- anybody who is occasionally too busy or too tired to feel like cooking (that includes me!).

How can non-cooks make sure that they are well nourished? One way is to use the very simple recipes and ideas in this chapter, and also those in the non-cooks' chapter in the companion volume *Easy Cooking for One or Two*.

Once you have mastered them, you might like to try some of the simple recipes in other chapters, e.g.:

When you don't feel like cooking at all, you could make use of foods which are sold ready to eat. But do be careful in your choice – some are poor value for money. I am thinking particularly of some of the pasties, pies and ready-to-eat desserts I have tried lately – far too expensive for what they contain, poor nourishment, and some quite disgusting in flavour!

Still, nothing venture, nothing gain – you will find some good buys in many shops.

Note that all the items listed below can be bought ready to eat in one- or two-portion sizes. Some come from the grocer, delicatessen or supermarket; some are prepared by the take-away cook shop (a few come from either shop or cook shop so I have put them in both lists). Some of the foods are eaten cold, some just need heating through.

My 'spies' over the British Isles have reported on some of their favourite regional ready-to-eat foods. So do not expect to find everything on the list in your local shops. On the other hand, you may find other ready-to-eat foods not included in this list. For instance, there is now a large range of one- or two-portion canned, frozen and packet foods too numerous to mention. The lists below are merely a guide, just intended to whet your appetite.

You may like to underline the foods you would like to

try, ring round those you might like to try, and cross out any you are certain you would not wish to try. If someone else does the shopping for you, show your marked list to them – it will guide them in their choice.

Take-away Foods

Fish and chips
Fried chicken and chips
Pie and chips
Hamburgers
Barbecue spare ribs
Pizza
Meat pies, sausage rolls
Scotch eggs

Jellied eels
Salads
Sandwiches
Vegetarian flans, pasties
International 'take aways',
    e.g. Chinese, Indian,
    Greek
Hot apple turnovers

Ready to Eat from Grocer, Greengrocer, Delicatessen or Supermarket

Sliced meats, luxury, e.g.
    ox tongue, roast beef,
    smoked beef, salami
Sliced meats, cheaper, e.g.
    luncheon sausage,
    brawn, liver sausage
Saveloys, 'savoury ducks',
    faggots, viennas,
    frankfurters, black
    puddings
Cold cooked chicken

Individual pies, e.g. pork,
    steak and kidney
Cold veal and ham pie
Pasties, sausage rolls
Scotch eggs
Tripe (sold ready to eat
    in some districts)
Pâtés, e.g. liver, duckling,
    salmon spread, potted
    meat
Individual pizzas

Smoked herrings, e.g. roll mops, buckling; smoked mackerel or trout

Smoked cod's roe or taramasalata

Flans, e.g. lentil, spinach; quiches

Ready-made sandwiches or rolls

Cartons of vegetable salad, e.g. coleslaw, potato, egg salad

A wide variety of cheeses, including local cheeses

A wide variety of breads and scones, including oat cakes

A wide variety of biscuits, savoury or sweet

Cheesecakes or gateaux, in individual slices

Syllabub, fruit jelly, trifles

Fruit pies, custard tarts

Yogurts

Fresh fruits

Baked Apples

Note. Because cooking apples are sometimes expensive, this recipe economizes by cutting each one in half – and cooking is quick so it saves on fuel too.

Serves 1 or 2 (if serving 1, the second half of the baked apple can be eaten cold next day)

Oven temperature: 400°F, gas mark 6

Cooking time: approximately 15–20 minutes

INGREDIENTS

1 medium to large cooking apple   a little water

Suggested fillings

(a) demerara sugar and butter
  or
(b) mincemeat
  or
(c) any dried fruit (e.g. sultanas, currants) and butter
  or
(d) small squares of plain chocolate broken from a chocolate bar

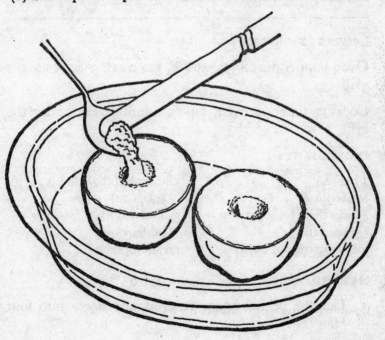

METHOD

1   Cut across in half, without peeling, and cut out centre core with a knife or corer.
2   Stand apples in an ovenproof dish with a little water.
3   Fill with your chosen filling. Cover dish.
4   Bake at 400°F, gas mark 6, till soft – approximately 15–20 minutes, depending on size and variety of apple. Watch to avoid overcooking.

Banana Pinwheels

Serves 2 (2 rolls each)

Oven temperature: 375–400°F, gas mark 5–6, or use the grill

Cooking time: in oven, 10–15 minutes; less under the grill

INGREDIENTS

1 banana
lemon juice
4 large slices bread, crusts removed
soft margarine or butter

cinnamon (about half a teaspoon)
granulated sugar (about 2 tablespoons)
cream (optional)

METHOD

1   Cut the peeled banana across and down into four 'fingers'.

2 Sprinkle with lemon juice.
3 Spread generously one side of each slice of bread with soft margarine or butter.
4 Press a mixture of ground cinnamon and sugar on to the butter or margarine.
5 Place a banana finger on to the *unspread* side of each slice and roll up firmly.
6 Bake in oven at 375–400°F, gas mark 5–6, until the outside of the rolls are crisp and brown. Serve hot, with or without cream.

Grilled Banana Sandwich is a simple alternative. This is easier than the pinwheels, but not quite as decorative.

1 Put slices of banana, dipped in lemon juice, between two thin slices of bread.
2 Spread the *outsides* with soft margarine or butter, and cinnamon and sugar.
3 Toast both sides under a medium grill.

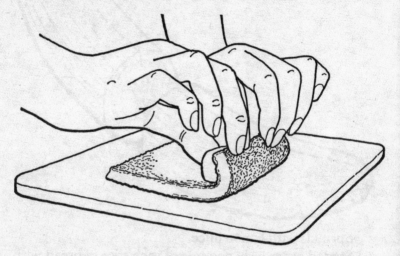

Note from test cooking. Recipe sent by Mrs E. G. Pegg from her 'Cooking for One' class in Nottingham. When made in class the unspread pinwheel is dipped in melted butter and then into the cinnamon and sugar – for a large quantity the extra trouble of melting butter would be worthwhile. A very popular recipe.

Bread and Milk

This is an economical dish, warming and comforting when you are not feeling up to eating more elaborate fare. It is best to use day-old, i.e. slightly stale, bread.

Serves 1

INGREDIENTS

1 cup of milk
1 slice of bread, about half an inch thick,
or
2 slices from a pre-sliced loaf
granulated sugar

METHOD

1   Bring the milk almost to the boil.
2   Meanwhile, cut the crusts from the bread and cut the bread into small cubes or squares. Put them in a serving bowl.
3   Sprinkle lightly with sugar (amount according to your taste).
4   Pour on the hot milk and 'sup with a spoon'.

Buckling

Serves 1 or more (allow half to one buckling per person, depending on appetite)

INGREDIENTS

buckling   horseradish cream
tomatoes   brown bread and butter

METHOD

Put the buckling on the serving plate with cut-up tomato or other favourite fresh salad. Good served with horseradish cream and eaten with bread and butter (if liked, with brown bread and butter).

Note. Buckling is a herring which has been smoked, whole and unsplit. During this process it becomes lightly cooked so it needs no further cooking. It is a rich fish with a delicate flavour. The bones quite easily come away from the flesh. Buckling can be bought at many delicatessen counters or at some fishmongers. Like all herrings, they are very nourishing.

Store-cupboard alternative. Use canned pilchards, horseradish cream and crispbread.

Cereals and Fruit

It used to be said that the main nourishment of breakfast cereals was the milk which was drunk with them! But now many varieties have added nutrients, particularly the valuable vitamins of the B group. One of the functions of these is to release energy from foods so that it can be used by the body. Some breakfast cereals also have iron added. It is quite an education to read the packet!

As fruits are more nourishing than sugar I suggest the following:

breakfast cereals   sliced banana
milk

Store-cupboard alternatives:

breakfast cereals
milk
dried fruits (sultanas, currants or mixed dried fruit)

or

canned sliced peaches (or other fruit)
a little of the fruit juice
a generous helping of All-bran sprinkled on top (eat while the
    All-bran is still crunchy)

Cheese Marmalade (toasted)

Sent by Mrs D. Smith of Gillingham, Kent – a *Yours* newspaper prizewinner.

Serves 1

INGREDIENTS

slice of bread
butter or margarine
marmalade

grated or thinly sliced
Cheddar cheese

METHOD

1 Toast a piece of bread on both sides.
2 Spread with butter or margarine on one side and then with marmalade.
3 Cover with grated or sliced cheese and return under the grill to melt the cheese.

Note from test cooking. Mrs Smith said that this may sound a funny mixture but people who have tried it agree that it is good. So we tried it – and thoroughly enjoyed it.

Cheese Marmalade (untoasted)

Even easier than the above recipe is a favourite of my father, an uncooked open sandwich:

1 Spread a slice of brown or white bread with a little butter or margarine.
2 Then spread thickly with cream cheese or a lactic cheese.
3 Finally spread with orange marmalade or orange and ginger marmalade. Cut in half.

Cinnamon Toast

On a cheerless, cold afternoon, warm yourself up with hot cinnamon toast and a cup of tea or a mug of hot cocoa.

INGREDIENTS

a slice or two of bread   ground cinnamon*
butter or margarine   granulated sugar*

* For 2 slices of bread you will need to mix about 1 tablespoon sugar with a good quarter of a teaspoon cinnamon.

METHOD

1 Toast the bread on one side only.
2 Spread the *un*toasted side thickly with butter or margarine.

3   Sprinkle liberally with ground cinnamon and granu-
    lated sugar.
4   Put back under the grill to toast – the sugar begins to
    melt and bubble in the heat.
5   Cut into four strips – if you are making these for a
    child, I wonder if they still call them 'soldiers'? – and
    serve them with a warming drink.

Cream Cheese Toast

Serves 2 (or 1 if hungry)

INGREDIENTS (to make two sandwiches)

4 slices brown or white bread
1 small packet (3-oz. size) Philadelphia cheese or cottage cheese
a little canned crushed pineapple
or
1 grated eating apple
or
1–2 teaspoons of your favourite pickle
salt and pepper
margarine

METHOD

1   Toast each slice on one side only. If you wish, remove
    crusts from bread.
2   Spread the *toasted* side of the bread with cheese, mixed
    with pineapple *or* grated apple *or* pickle. Season with
    salt and pepper unless using pickle.

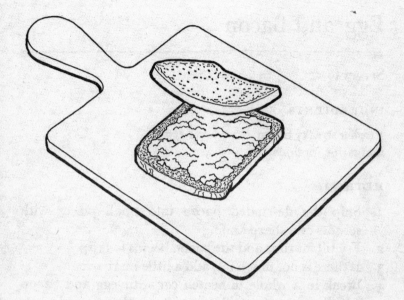

3 Press two slices together with the *untoasted* sides outside.
4 Spread one untoasted side with margarine and lay the sandwich, margarine side down, on the grill rack so that you can then spread the upper untoasted side with margarine.
5 Toast under a medium grill until golden brown on one side, turn (use a knife and fork to do this) and toast the other side. Serve immediately.

Comment from 'Meals for Pensioners' class, East Warwickshire College of Further Education, Rugby: 'We used cottage cheese bought already flavoured with pineapple.'

Egg and Bacon

Serves 1

INGREDIENTS

1 rasher streaky bacon   1 egg
margarine (optional)

METHOD

1 Snip the de-rinded bacon into small pieces with
   scissors or a sharp knife.
2 Fry till fat runs and the bacon begins to crisp.
3 If there is not much fat, add a little margarine.
4 Break in a whole unbeaten egg. Stir egg and bacon
   rapidly with a fork till it just sets – only a few minutes.

Eggs – Hard-boiled

(For soft, coddled eggs see *Easy Cooking for One or Two*,
pages 15–16.)

Some people put the eggs into a small saucepan of cold
water, bring it to the boil over medium heat and then
simmer it till cooked. But I find it difficult to judge exactly
when the boiling begins in order to time the eggs.

I prefer to lower the egg carefully into simmering (see

Glossary) water which covers it completely. Adjust the heat to keep the water steadily simmering and *for large eggs – simmer about 12 minutes, for smaller eggs – simmer about 10 minutes*. (The precise timing will depend on the degree of hardness you prefer.)

- Always remove eggs from the refrigerator at least an hour before you need them so that they regain room temperature before they are added to the simmering water.
- Should the egg crack, add a little salt to the water to prevent further leakage of the white.
- To avoid a black ring between the yolk and white of a hard-boiled egg (1) do not exceed the cooking time and (2) immediately the cooking time is up, run water from the cold tap over the egg.

Stuffed Eggs

Serves 1–2

INGREDIENTS

2 hard-boiled eggs (see previous recipe)
soft margarine
curry powder *or* Worcestershire sauce *or* tomato ketchup *or* a
    thick slice of liver sausage
salt and pepper

Can be served with tomato/lettuce and bread and butter.

METHOD

1 Cut each shelled hard-boiled egg into two lengthwise.
2 Scoop out the yolks and mash together with a little
   margarine and the chosen flavouring or the liver-
   sausage. You may find you need to add a little salt and
   pepper.
3 Pile the mixture back into the egg-white cases.

Fried Egg Sandwich

This is my favourite 'quickie' lunch or supper if I am
feeling peckish but too tired to make the effort to do more
than very simple cooking.

Serves 1

INGREDIENTS

butter, lard or bacon fat for   salt
   frying   tomato ketchup (optional)
1 egg per person
2 slices of buttered bread per
   person

METHOD

1 Heat a small knob of butter, lard or bacon fat in a

small frying pan until the butter begins to bubble; let lard or bacon fat heat for about half a minute after melting. It should then be hot enough to fry the egg without 'spitting' hot fat out of the pan.

2 Break the egg into the hot fat (a beginner may find it easier to break the egg first into a cup or saucer and then gently slide it into the fat).

3 When it is fried to your liking lift the egg (using a slice) carefully on to the first piece of buttered bread, placed on the plate. Sprinkle with a little salt and (if liked) tomato ketchup.

4 Press on the second piece of bread and butter to make a sandwich. Cut in quarters and eat, while good and hot, with knife and fork.

Notes from test cooking. Butter colours the whites golden, and flavours. Lard retains the egg whiteness, and flavours slightly; bacon fat colours golden brown and flavours.

If you like a soft yolk, fry for 2 or 3 minutes.

If you like a firm yolk you should fry longer – possibly up to 6 minutes.

If you like a brown, crisp edge to the white, increase the heat slightly.

If you like a glossy film, you can 'flip' some of the fat with a spoon over the yolk.

If you like your egg set on both sides, turn it over carefully with a slice (normally sold as a 'fish slice', see page 236).

Mandarin, Banana and Raisins

Serves 1–2

INGREDIENTS

1–2 bananas
1 small can mandarin oranges

a small handful of stoneless
raisins

METHOD

1   Slice the bananas (*Note:* if you are making this to last
    for 2 days, only cut up enough banana for 1 day at a
    time, otherwise it blackens on standing).
2   Mix them with the mandarin oranges, turned into a
    bowl. You will probably not need to use all the syrup,
    unless you have a real 'sweet-tooth', but make sure
    the bananas are moistened by the syrup.
3   Stir in the raisins.

Store-cupboard alternative. Instead of using fresh bananas,
mix canned grapefruit segments with the mandarin
oranges and raisins. This will probably make enough for
3 or 4 servings – it can be kept for 2 days.

MILK DRINKS
Hot Chocolate Brandy (or Rum)

One or two milky drinks a day – elevenses or nightcaps –
form the basis of a good daily diet. Some time ago –
working in consultation with the National Dairy Council
– I sent twenty tested milk drinks to 'Over 60s' and
'Retirement' cookery classes up and down the country.
This was one of the favourites:

Serves 1

INGREDIENTS

1 cup hot milk
2 heaped teaspoons drinking
  chocolate

3 teaspoons brandy *or* 2
  teaspoons rum

METHOD

1 Pour the hot milk into a cup.
2 Quickly stir in drinking chocolate and brandy or rum.

Ovaltine

This is a comforting nightcap, and nourishing. Ovaltine
has vitamin D added to it, so is particularly recommended
if you are housebound or do not get out much into the

sunlight (sunlight gives your body vitamin D). Look at the labels of other milk-drink ingredients to see whether they, too, have additional vitamin D.

Serves 1

INGREDIENTS

1 cup hot (or ice-cold) milk   2 heaped teaspoons (or to taste) Ovaltine

METHOD

1 Pour the hot milk into the cup and quickly stir in the Ovaltine to dissolve.
2 In summer you may prefer refreshing cold Ovaltine. Pour ice-cold milk into a glass or cup – not too full. Sprinkle on the Ovaltine and whisk it briskly with a fork so that it slightly dissolves – the rest is left on top, pleasantly crunchy.

Hot Mocha Milk

Serves 1

INGREDIENTS

1 cup milk   1 heaped teaspoon drinking
half a teaspoon instant coffee   chocolate

METHOD

1 Bring the milk almost to the boil.

2 Pour into the cup and stir in the coffee and chocolate till dissolved. You can vary the amounts of coffee and chocolate according to taste.

Spanish Onion – Boiled

Onions are not very nourishing, but some folk swear by boiled onions as a cure for a cold. Whatever you think, this is certainly a comforting simple supper for a cold night!

INGREDIENTS

1 large Spanish (mild) onion   butter
   per person   wholemeal bread and butter
salt

METHOD

1 In a saucepan with a tightly fitting lid, bring plenty of water to a fast boil, with a teaspoon or so of salt.
2 Peel the onion but leave whole. Lower gently into the water.
3 Put on the lid, and reduce the heat so that the onion boils gently till tender (about 30–40 minutes, depending on size). Test by piercing with a sharp knife so that you can feel whether the onion is soft enough.
4 Lift out and drain off the water. Put on a plate with a large knob of butter, and eat with knife and fork. I like this with a slice of wholemeal bread and butter.

Potato Baked in Its Jacket

Serves 1

Oven temperature: 400°F, gas mark 6

Cooking time: 45 minutes to 1 hour

INGREDIENTS

1 medium potato (about   a little butter or margarine
   4–6 oz.)

METHOD

1   Scrub the potato in water to remove all soil. Pat dry.
2   Prick the skin all over with a fork (this prevents the
    skin bursting in the heat of the oven).
3   Rub the skin with a little butter or margarine (it
    saves mess if you rub with the paper from the packet –
    it generally has some butter or margarine stuck to it).
4   Bake on the middle oven shelf at 400°F, gas mark 6 till
    the potato feels soft when gently pinched (to avoid
    burns you may like to use an oven glove kept well
    away from the gas or electric heat – pinch the potato
    gently otherwise you may burst it). A medium-sized
    potato is generally baked to perfection in 45 minutes
    to 1 hour.

Cheese and Chutney Jacket Potato

When the potato has been baked in its jacket, cut it in half and mash into it some butter or margarine, and some grated cheese mixed with your favourite chutney or pickle.

Cheese and Chives Jacket Potato

When the potato has been baked in its jacket, cut it in half and mash into it some cottage cheese flavoured with chives, or a portion of Boursin cheese.

Rhubarb and Lemon

Serves 2–3

INGREDIENTS

1 lb. rhubarb   a little sugar to taste
1 lemon

METHOD

1   Wash and cut up the rhubarb into half- to one-inch lengths and place in saucepan. (If you want to make it more mellow, pour on some boiling water, let it

stand for 5 minutes and then pour off the water. This is not essential but I generally do it.)

2   Remove all the peel and pith and pips from the lemon and cut the flesh into small pieces.

3   Add the lemon to the rhubarb with only a tablespoon or two of water, and – with the lid on the pan – cook very gently till tender.

4   Sweeten to taste, but keep it sharp and tangy so that it is thirst-quenching when cold.

Rich Cheese Dessert

Serves 1

INGREDIENTS

1 or 2 pots Gervais full-fat cheese
1 teaspoon sour cream
or
top of the milk or single cream
ground cinnamon
1 plump sweetened dried apricot*
or
1 teaspoon mixed dried fruit

   * These special apricots are obtainable from some stores and health-food shops.

METHOD

1   Turn out the cheese into a small serving bowl or plate.

2 Add the sour cream or top of the milk or single cream.
3 Sprinkle liberally with cinnamon.
4 Eat with the apricot (which is a real luxury) or – almost as nice – the dried fruit. The cheese mixture sprinkled with dried fruit is eaten with a spoon, but it is easier to pick up the apricot with the fingers.

Roll Mop Salad

Serves 1 or more – allow 1–2 roll mops per person, depending on appetite

INGREDIENTS

roll mops
potato salad (ready-prepared, or home-made)

1 red-skinned apple (optional)
cucumber

METHOD

Put the drained roll mop on the plate with a little potato salad, into which you can cut up some unpeeled red apple. Serve with slices of cucumber.

Note. Roll mops are filleted herrings which have been soaked in spiced vinegar. They are generally rolled up with onions, gherkins and peppercorns. They can be bought in jars or, at some delicatessen counters, are sold separately. Like all herrings, they are very nourishing.

Store-cupboard alternative. Canned tuna or canned mackerel, with canned vegetable salad.

Sandwiches

I know some people worry because their elderly relatives are 'only eating sandwiches'. But what is wrong with sandwiches? They are an easy-to-make food, and very nourishing, especially if the fillings are tempting and well chosen. Here are a few ideas. You will probably have many more of your own:

Cheddar cheese and chutney or pickle

Cottage cheese and chopped dates

Cottage cheese and celery

Marmite (yeast extract) and (plenty of) chopped parsley

Yeast extract and chopped walnuts

Tomato, cucumber and chopped watercress

Sardine and tomato mashed with lemon juice and seasoned with pepper

Peanut butter and fresh sliced cucumber

Ham and tomato, or ham and pickle

Rather expensive, but very nourishing: smoked cod's roe and cress (less expensive: a little smoked cod's roe mixed with cottage cheese)

Sliced banana and honey between two slices of wholemeal bread

Hard-boiled egg mashed with mayonnaise *or* with top
of milk, salt, pepper, mustard and chives or parsley

Ploughman's Lunch

A hunk of bread (e.g. French bread), a pat of butter or
margarine, a wedge of your favourite cheese, a pickled
onion or a gherkin or a spoonful of pickle, a raw tomato
or other salad vegetable.

Dagwood

This may sound extravagant, but it is in fact a meal in
itself and my way of making very little go a long way. You
can vary the ingredients according to your larder. For
each person, use three slices of brown or white bread.
Spread lightly with butter or margarine, then spread one
with yeast extract, add a leaf or two of lettuce, sliced
tomato, scraps of meat (e.g. cooked beef, lamb, chicken
or ham). Add the second slice of buttered bread, then
sliced egg or cheese moistened with mayonnaise or a little
Russian salad or coleslaw, more lettuce or cucumber and
a final topping of buttered bread. Press it firmly together
and slice into two or four.

Toasted Sandwiches

For example:

Banana Pin Wheels or Sandwich, pages 6, 7
Cream Cheese Toast, page 14
Hot Sardine Toast, page 32
Sardine or Paste Rolls, pages 33, 35

Scandinavian Open Sandwiches

For example: one slice of buttered bread, topped with a slice of luncheon meat, a spoonful of cottage cheese and decorated with a twist of sliced orange. (Eat the rest of the orange for dessert.)

Sandwiches with Hot Cooked Fillings

For example: Fried Egg Sandwich, page 18.

Salad Sandwiches

These are particularly nice between two slices of whole-meal bread:

fill with lettuce, tomato, celery or watercress; or with carrot, lemon juice and currants (see page 97).

REMEMBER THERE IS A WIDE RANGE OF BREADS — these can add as much variety to your sandwiches as the fillings. Try rye bread, black bread, brown bread (if you want high fibre in your diet, don't just ask for 'brown', ask for wholemeal), milk breads, baps and other soft rolls, crisp rolls, crispbreads, crackers ...

SANDWICHES ARE AT THEIR BEST SERVED WITH a

piece of fruit, a glass of milk or a vitamin C drink, a beer or some other favourite drink.

Hot Sardine Toast

Sent by Miss D. A. Stocks, Barrow-in-Furness – a prize-winner in the *Yours* newspaper competition.

Serves 1

INGREDIENTS

2 slices of toast
1 small tin sardines

pepper and lemon juice
(optional)

METHOD

1 Place the mashed sardines (mash them, if you like, with pepper and lemon juice) between the slices of hot toast. There is no need to butter the toast.

2 Keep the grill turned low – or you may be able to turn off the grill after toasting the bread – and place the fish sandwich under the warm grill for about 2 or 3 minutes to heat through. This is nourishing and makes a tasty meal at tea-time.

Notes from test cooking. This is a small, simple variation on the popular snack Sardines on Toast. In Hot Sardine Toast the sardines are made into a sandwich and are comfortingly warm instead of cold. Serve with a steaming hot mug of tea or coffee.

For extra flavour we added a little pepper and plenty of lemon juice to the sardines, but this is not essential. For extra nourishment (calcium and vitamin D needed for strong bones) mash the sardine bones in with the fish.

Sardine Rolls

Serves 2

INGREDIENTS

6 slices bread
butter or margarine for
    spreading

1 can sardines
a little pepper
lemon juice

Can be served with quartered tomatoes or slices of cucumber.

METHOD

1   Remove crusts from bread and slightly flatten each slice, using the blade of the knife.

2   Spread with butter or margarine.
3   Mash the sardines (drained from their oil) with

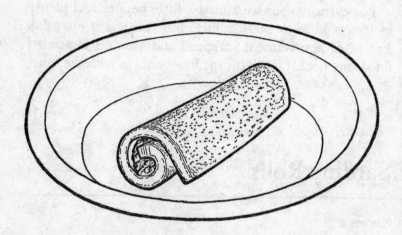

pepper and lemon juice to flavour. Spread on the
bread.
4   Roll up each slice, pressing to make a roll. Place on
the grill pan. Spread the top carefully with softened
margarine or butter.
5   Brown under the grill.
6   Turn the rolls over, spread with a little more margarine or butter and brown the untoasted side under
the grill.

These tasty rolls can be eaten with knife and fork, or fingers.

Store-cupboard alternative. Spread with paste instead of sardines.

Spiced Orange

If you find oranges troublesome to peel, or if you feel that they taste too acid eaten raw, try this simple method for serving a sweetened, warmed orange for dessert. Heat it for 3–5 minutes and eat it straight away; that way you retain most of the vitamin C.

Serves 1–2

INGREDIENTS

1 large orange
1 teaspoon brown sugar

a good pinch of mixed spice
margarine

METHOD

1 Halve the orange and, if necessary, cut a small sliver of skin from the bottom of each half to make it stand properly.
2 Loosen the segments with a sharp knife.
3 Sprinkle the brown sugar and mixed spice over the fruit and dot with small knobs of margarine.
4 Place under the grill – near enough to the heat to

warm but not too near so that it burns. Heat 3–5 minutes, until just warmed through.

Note from test cooking. This was tested in a 'Cookery for the Blind' class at Haywards Heath Adult Education Centre, Sussex. They found it was a good idea to loosen the segments before grilling.

Spicy Gruel

Nourishing and cheap. (It is slightly misnamed because true gruel is a thin form of porridge made with oats, barley or other cereals. This one uses flour like a sauce – it is much quicker to make.)

Serves 1

INGREDIENTS

quarter of a pint milk
half an oz. margarine
half an oz. plain flour

for flavouring: a knob of butter or margarine, ground cinnamon, granulated sugar

METHOD

1 Place the milk, margarine and flour in a small saucepan, stir and leave without cooking for a minute or two so that the flour begins to soften in the milk.
2 With a wooden spoon stir constantly over gentle heat

until the margarine melts and the sauce comes to the boil and thickens.

3   Pour into a warmed cereal bowl.
4   Serve immediately, with a knob of butter or margarine melting into it. Sprinkle generously with cinnamon and sugar to taste.

Substantial Soup

Serves 2

INGREDIENTS

1 cooked potato (left-over)
1 or 2 *cooked* sausages or
   frankfurters
1 can lentil soup (or home-
   made Lentil Soup, see page
   82)

a little milk
wedge of lemon, or chopped
   parsley (optional)

METHOD

1   Cut up the potato and cooked sausages.
2   Heat through in the soup, adding a little milk if the soup is very thick.
3   If liked, serve with a wedge of lemon to squeeze into the soup, or with chopped parsley sprinkled on top.

Uncooked Cheesecake

Serves 1

INGREDIENTS

ginger cake or a moist   top of the milk
   gingerbread (shop-bought)   red jam
curd cheese

METHOD

1 Cut a slice from the ginger cake.
2 Soften some curd cheese by mashing it with top of the
   milk, to make it easy to spread.
3 Spread very thickly on top of the ginger cake. Decorate with a little jam.

Chapter 2
'Yours'

Some time ago I was asked to write a cookery supplement for *Yours*, the newspaper which is produced by 'Help the Aged' for readers of retirement age. (For details, write to Distribution Department, *Yours*, P.O. Box 30, London NI IRF.)

I suggested that it would be more fun to run a competition asking for readers' favourite recipes. With their consent, the prizewinners' recipes are reprinted below.

Then I heard that three Home Economics Diploma students (Linda Garnier, Jennifer Harris and Valery Urquhart) at Queen Margaret College, Edinburgh, had been given a special assignment: 'To devise recipes which you consider pensioners would enjoy.' They, too, have given me permission to reprint a selection from their easy-to-cook recipes – enjoyed by the students as well as the pensioners.

Bacon and Green Beans

Sent by Mrs A. L. Trenchard of Surbiton, Surrey.

Serves 1 or more

INGREDIENTS

runner or dwarf beans   rashers of bacon

METHOD

1   Take as many beans, runner or dwarf, as required.
2   Wash and string them and boil in salted water until tender.
3   Strain, and put the beans into a heatproof casserole dish.
4   Take as many rashers of bacon as required, lay them on the beans and stand the casserole under the grill with moderate heat until cooked.

Notes from test cooking. Because beans were not yet in season when this recipe was tested we used frozen sliced runner beans. We bought the cheapest streaky rashers of bacon and the result was delicious.

Bacon and Potatoes

Sent by Mr Stanley F. Bright of Tiverton, Devon.
Serves 1

INGREDIENTS

1 medium-to-large potato per person

2 rashers bacon per person

seasoning

METHOD

1 Take one good-sized potato for each person. Wash, peel and slice fairly thinly.

2 Place in a frying pan and half cover with cold water. Bring to the boil and turn over the potatoes once or twice, and then cover with a large enamel plate or a lid to keep in the steam and shorten cooking time. Keep the water boiling *gently* until the potatoes are nearly cooked.

3 When nearly cooked lift the plate or lid and place 2 rashers of bacon for each person on top of the potatoes. Replace the lid. In a few minutes time the bacon will be 'cooked a treat' and boiled, of course, which is more palatable than fried bacon.

4 Serve with pepper and, if necessary, salt to taste.

Notes from test cooking. Mr Bright suggested using an enamel plate so that if it is too hot on removal it will not break if dropped! But instead we found a saucepan lid which fitted our frying pan adequately. It is advisable to peep from time to time to see that the potatoes are not boiling dry. We found that as the bacon was slightly salty we did not need to add any salt, just pepper. The flavour of potato and bacon mingled in a most appetizing way.

Bacon Pudding

Sent by Miss S. R. Brightmer, Lee-on-Solent, Hampshire.

Serves 2–3

Cooking time: steam for 2 hours 30 minutes to 3 hours *or* bake at 400°F, gas mark 6, for 1 hour 30 minutes

INGREDIENTS

Suet pastry	*Filling*
6 oz. self-raising flour*	half a lb. bacon pieces
3 oz. shredded suet	1 onion, chopped finely
pinch salt	1 teaspoon mixed herbs
	a little water

  * Or use 6 oz. plain flour with 3 level teaspoons baking powder.

METHOD

1 Mix the flour and suet together, add a pinch of salt and a little water and knead to a firm dough (see page 145 for suet pastry method).

2 Roll out the pastry and line a basin, leaving a piece of dough to cover the top of the pudding.

3 Cut the bacon into small pieces and place in the lined pudding basin with chopped onion and mixed herbs. Add a little water.

4 Roll out the piece of extra left-over dough for the top crust and place the pastry lid on top of the filling, brushing with water and pressing to seal.

5 Cover with greaseproof paper tied with string (or cover with foil) and place in a steamer until cooked. (You can steam in a saucepan with the boiling water coming about a third of the way up the basin – see Glossary, page 242.)

Notes from test cooking. Because we find that some people have difficulty in lifting puddings in and out of a steamer, we baked this pudding very successfully at 400°F, gas mark 6, covered with foil, for 1 hour 30 minutes.

Beef Layer Pie

Sent by Mrs E. Davies of Newport, Salop.

Serves 2 good portions

Oven temperature: 350°F, gas mark 4

Cooking time: 1 hour

INGREDIENTS

1 small onion, finely chopped   4 tablespoons water or stock
half an oz. dripping   salt and pepper
half a lb. minced beef   dash Worcestershire sauce
half a level tablespoon flour

Suet pastry

3 oz. self-raising flour *   pinch salt
one and a half oz. shredded   little water to mix
  suet

* Or use 3 oz. plain flour with one and a half level teaspoons
baking powder.

METHOD

1 Make the pastry by mixing the flour, suet and salt
   with enough water to make a medium firm dough (see
   page 145 for suet pastry method).
2 Fry onion lightly in dripping.
3 Add mince and stir over heat until well browned.
4 Mix in the flour, stock, seasoning and Worcestershire
   sauce.
5 Roll pastry thinly into 2 rounds – or shapes to fit your
   heatproof dish.
6 Spoon half the meat into a heatproof dish; cover with
   a pastry layer; spoon the rest of the meat on top of the
   pastry; cover with the second pastry layer.
7 Cover with greased kitchen foil and bake at 350°F, gas
   mark 4, for 1 hour.

Notes from test cooking. We used a small piece of stock

cube with water to make the stock and added a *good* dash Worcestershire sauce for flavouring.

Boiled Fruit Cake

Sent by Mrs Norfolk of Chelmsford, Essex.

A very similar recipe came from Mrs Holt of St Albans, Hertfordshire. Mrs Holt makes the remark that she feels many elderly or handicapped readers may be unable to cream fat and sugar or to rub fat and flour together easily and as this is a boiled cake, which only needs stirring, she thinks it is particularly easy to mix.

Oven temperature: 300–325°F, gas mark 2–3

Cooking time: approximately 1 hour 30 minutes

INGREDIENTS

8 oz. sultanas
4 oz. glacé cherries } or 12 oz. mixed dried fruit
4 oz. margarine
4 oz. sugar
quarter of a pint cold water
2 medium eggs or 1 large egg, beaten
8 oz. self-raising flour (or use plain flour, plus 1 level teaspoon baking powder)
small pinch salt

You will need a 6- or 7-inch cake tin or a loaf tin, greased.

You may find it easier to turn out if you line the bottom
of the tin with greased, greaseproof paper.

METHOD

1   Put into a saucepan the fruit, margarine, sugar and
    water. Heat, and when the margarine is melted,
    simmer slowly for 20 minutes, stirring occasionally.
2   Allow to cool.
3   When nearly cold, add to the saucepan the eggs and
    flour and salt. Stir well in.
4   Turn into the greased and lined tin. If the mixture
    looks pink when the flour is put in, it will be all right;
    it will turn brown when cooked.
5   Bake in a slow oven 300–325°F, gas mark 2–3, for
    about 1 hour 30 minutes.

   Notes from test cooking. When it is cooked it will be firm
to the touch and will be shrinking away a little from the
tin. A skewer pushed into it will come out clean (if it is
*under*cooked, sticky raw mixture coats the skewer).

Bread, Cheese and Nut Pudding

Sent by Miss M. Ellis of Ipswich, Suffolk.

Serves 2

Oven temperature: 400°F, gas mark 6

Cooking time: 50 minutes

INGREDIENTS

Amounts depend on size of pie dish, so the following quantities are approximate:

5 slices slightly stale bread from a small loaf
2 oz. cheese
one third of a pint of milk

1 oz. margarine
1 egg
pepper and salt
chopped nuts

METHOD

1 Fill a greased pie dish with bread broken into small pieces.
2 Add cheese to taste (either small pieces or grated).
3 Add a mixture of warm milk, margarine and beaten egg, seasoned with pepper and salt.
4 Dot the top with chopped nuts (any variety from peanuts to the more expensive walnut pieces can be used).
5 Bake 40 minutes at 400°F, gas mark 6, with the dish covered by foil. To get a crisp top bake a further 10 minutes minus the foil.

Notes from test cooking. We had several excellent recipes sent in for bread and cheese puddings, but we chose this one because it did not call for grating the bread or cheese. Moreover, the chopped nuts on top gave it interest.

At step 3 we warmed the milk with the margarine but did not make it too hot, took it off the heat and carefully beat in the egg and seasoning.

We found some broken almonds which were being sold cheaply but, as Miss Ellis says, any variety of nuts can be used. They should be chopped into small pieces.

Bready Omelette

Sent by Mrs I. F. Bowles of Crawley, Sussex.

Serves 1 for lunch – or 2 for breakfast with bacon

INGREDIENTS

half-inch-thick slice of white
  bread from a large loaf
2 tablespoons milk

1 egg
pepper and salt
fat for frying

METHOD

1 Remove crusts and crumble the bread into a basin.
2 Add milk and with a fork beat into a paste.
3 Add egg and seasonings and beat all together.
4 Fry in hot fat, turning when set firm enough, 2–3 minutes.

Notes from test cooking. Fried in lard or butter, very good, but in bacon fat, delicious! Can be varied with the addition of chopped chives or a little chopped ham.
  This recipe makes the most of one egg.

We served Bready Omelette with the recipe for Bacon and Green Beans sent in by Mrs Trenchard (page 40) and the two together made a satisfying and attractive lunch.

Cheese Soufflé

Sent by Mrs H. Poole of Southbourne, Bournemouth, Hampshire.

Serves 2; halve quantities for 1

Oven temperature: 325°F, gas mark 3

Cooking time: approximately 45 minutes

INGREDIENTS

1 pint milk
2 oz. semolina (or ground rice)
2 eggs, separated

salt, pepper and mustard
small onion, grated, to taste
4 oz. cheese, grated

METHOD

1 Cook the semolina for 2 minutes in the milk. Cool.
2 Beat in the egg yolks with the seasonings, onion and grated cheese.
3 When ready to cook, whisk up the whites of egg and fold in.
4 Put in a greased, straight-sided dish at the top of a

preheated oven, 325°F, gas mark 3, for about 45 minutes.

Notes from test cooking. This is a very light, easily digested way of eating cheese. It makes a satisfying dish and half quantities are enough for one person.

Date Cake

Sent by a *Yours* newspaper reader from Yorkshire.

Oven temperature: 300°F, gas mark 2

Cooking time: approximately 1 hour 30 minutes

INGREDIENTS

3 oz. cooking dates
4 oz. self-raising flour
2 oz. soft margarine
one and a half oz. sugar

half a teaspoon bicarbonate
    of soda
milk (may not be needed)

Size of round tin used: 6–7 inches in diameter. You could use a loaf tin. Grease the tin but there is no need to line it with paper.

METHOD

1 Put the dates in a breakfast cup and just cover them with boiling water. Mash them around with a fork. Do not drain off the water.

2 Transfer to a larger basin and add all the other ingredients. Stir together, adding a little milk if not soft enough.
3 Turn into the greased tin. Bake at 300°F, gas mark 2, until firm to the touch and brown and a skewer comes out clean (approximately 1 hour 30 minutes).

Notes from test cooking. Having added the water with the dates we found we did not need any milk to mix this cake to a dropping consistency (see Glossary, page 235).

Because we used soft margarine there was no need to rub in; it mixed very easily with a wooden spoon.

Egg Nest

Sent by Mrs M. Rigby of Newcastle upon Tyne.

Serves 1

Oven temperature: 350–375°F, gas mark 4–5

Cooking time: about 15 minutes

INGREDIENTS

butter or margarine
about 2 tablespoons grated
  cheese

1 egg per person
pepper and salt
toast or bread and butter

METHOD

1 Sprinkle half the grated cheese in a buttered small
   ovenproof dish.
2 Break an egg on top
3 Season very lightly
4 Cover with the remaining grated cheese.
5 Bake in a moderate oven until set. Eat with toast or
   bread and butter.

Notes from test cooking. We used an old china saucer in
place of an ovenproof dish and found that the egg took 15
minutes to set to our liking. This is an ideal recipe to
make best use of oven space if you are already cooking a
cake or other dishes in a moderate oven.

Fish Crumble with Sauce

Sent by Mrs Olwen Lewis of Llanymynech, Mont-
gomeryshire.

Serves 2 or 3

Oven temperature: 400°F, gas mark 6

Cooking time: approximately 35 minutes

INGREDIENTS

1 or 2 potatoes (optional)   salt and pepper
2 or 3 fillets of white fish   a knob of butter or margarine
lemon juice

Topping

two and a half oz. margarine   2 oz. grated or crumbled
5 oz. plain flour   cheese

Serve with apple or parsley sauce and oven baked potatoes – see below.

METHOD

1 If you are serving potatoes, prepare them first and put them in the oven as it is heating up (see below).
2 Grease an ovenproof dish and lay the fish fillets on the bottom, overlapping if necessary.
3 Sprinkle with plenty of lemon juice, season lightly and dot with pieces of butter or margarine.
4 Prepare topping by rubbing the two and a half oz. margarine into the flour; add seasoning and stir in grated or crumbled cheese.
5 Sprinkle the topping over the fish and bake, covered, at 400°F, gas mark 6, for 20 minutes.
6 Remove the cover from the dish (and from the potatoes if you are cooking them at the same time) and continue cooking until the crumble begins to turn pale golden, and the potatoes are tender and crisp (about another 15 minutes).
7 Meanwhile, make an apple sauce in your usual way by puréeing apples but adding the grated rind of half a lemon and a little lemon juice (or you can buy a small can of apple sauce). *Or* make a one-stage parsley sauce (p. 129–30) *or* make up a parsley sauce

mix according to packet directions. (Fish crumble is
at its best served with a sauce.)

To make oven-baked potatoes: (a) before beginning to
prepare the fish, put 1 or 2 potatoes, peeled and thickly
sliced, on to a greased ovenproof plate, (b) season lightly
and cover with greased greaseproof paper, (c) remove the
paper to brown the potatoes when you uncover the fish
at step 6. If they look dry at this stage, dot them with a
little margarine or butter.

Fish Pie

Sent by Mrs C. Chapman of Eltham, SE9 (who says that
she finds it convenient to use the oven). But this is all
cooked on top of the stove and then (if you like) browned
under the grill so that it is not necessary to use the oven.

Serves 2 for the first day – the remainder of the pie can be
reheated gently for another meal for 2 the next day

INGREDIENTS

three-quarters of a lb. fresh   2 tomatoes, skinned and
   coley or smoked haddock   chopped
1 hard-boiled egg, sliced or   seasoning
   chopped

Sauce

1 oz. margarine   half a pint milk
1 oz. flour   2 oz. cheese, grated

Topping

1 lb. potatoes, boiled ⎫
chopped parsley   ⎪ or a small packet of instant potato
milk   ⎬ and a little chopped parsley
margarine   ⎪
seasoning   ⎭

METHOD

1 Make cheese sauce – for one-stage method, see page 129.
2 Poach the fish in a little milk or milk and water. Remove skin and bones when it is cooked.
3 Add egg and tomatoes and flaked fish to the sauce. Stir over low heat to heat through.
4 Pour into a greased pie dish or casserole.
5 Mash the hot potatoes with parsley, milk, margarine and seasoning to make creamed potatoes, and fork over the top of the casserole (or use reconstituted packet potato mixed with a little chopped parsley).
6 Optional: dot with a few flakes of margarine and brown under the grill.

Notes from test cooking. The drawback is that you need several saucepans for the preparation, so we thought it might prove too troublesome; but the result was good – worth the fuss!

To make it easy, you could divide the preparation into two sessions: Cook and flake the fish, and boil the egg earlier in the day. Once that is cleared up, make the sauce and mash the potatoes (or use the instant mash) just before you are ready for lunch or dinner.

The instant mash (reconstituted as given in the packet directions) was rather solid for spreading over the pie, so we softened it by adding some of the milk in which the fish was poached (to poach: see Glossary, page 238).

Hamburger Quickie

Sent by Mrs M. H. Farr of Warley, Worcestershire.

Makes 6 hamburgers – enough for 2 servings

INGREDIENTS

half a lb. raw minced beef   fat for frying
1 packet onion soup

Serve with vegetables.

METHOD

1   Mix 1 tablespoon of the onion soup powder with the minced beef.
2   Form into six rounds on a floured board, and flatten slightly.
3   Fry in a little hot fat until brown on both sides.

4   Mix the remainder of the soup powder with three-quarters of a pint cold water, bring to the boil and carefully pour over the meat in the frying pan.
5   Cover with a lid and simmer for 25 minutes.
6   Serve with mashed potatoes and peas or other vegetables according to taste.

Notes from test cooking. If you want to eat three of these on one day and three the next, cool the ones you are keeping rapidly by standing the pan in cold water. Store them in the cold – a refrigerator if possible – and next day reheat them *very* thoroughly, allowing at least 5 minutes boiling before eating them.

Ham and Leek (or Celery) Mornay

Sent by Mrs M. E. Seymour of Whitney-on-Wye, Herefordshire.

Serves 2

Oven temperature: 400°F, gas mark 6

Cooking time: approximately 20–30 minutes

INGREDIENTS
a little grated or crumbled cheese
2 slices cooked ham
2 small leeks, well trimmed, washed and boiled,

or
2 celery hearts (canned)
or
2–3 sticks fresh celery, cut in short lengths and boiled

Sauce
half a pint white or cheese sauce (One-stage Sauce, page 129,
   or
   half a pint of packet sauce)

METHOD

1 Sprinkle a little grated or crumbled cheese into a pie
   dish.
2 Wrap pieces of ham round boiled leeks or drained
   celery and place on cheese.
3 Make the sauce (for the liquid you can use a mixture
   of milk and leek water).
4 Pour over the ham parcels.
5 Sprinkle a little grated or crumbled cheese on top.
6 Bake in the oven at 400°F, gas mark 6, for about 20–
   30 minutes.

Notes from test cooking. Celery hearts can be bought in
cans but there may be too many for your use unless you
cook them for another meal. Leeks are an economical
alternative.
   This is a filling dish but if you like you can eat it with
potatoes, sweetcorn or plain strips of toast.

Lamb's Kidneys or Liver

Sent by Mrs M. McGegan of West Bridgford, Nottingham.

Serves 2 people, or makes 1 serving one day and 1 serving the next

INGREDIENTS

4 oz. lamb's liver or 3 lamb's kidneys

1 onion

1 oz. fat or oil

2 oz. bacon pieces

2 oz. mushrooms, sliced

1 sliced tomato (fresh or canned)

or

1 teaspoon tomato purée seasoning

good pinch mixed herbs

1 teaspoon flour and half a cup milk (optional)

Can be served with mashed potato or boiled rice.

METHOD

1 Wash the liver or kidneys (cut out and discard the white core from the kidneys) and cut into small pieces.

2 Chop onion and fry lightly; add bacon.

3 Put in liver or kidney and stir with wooden spoon for 5 minutes to fry lightly.

4 Add mushrooms, tomato and seasoning, and sprinkle in herbs. Cover and cook for 10 minutes on a very low heat.

5 If you want more gravy, blend half a cup milk
   slowly into 1 teaspoon flour, and stir into mixture for
   a few minutes.

Notes from test cooking. We made this with lamb's kidneys and we did make the gravy at the end with the flour
and milk. It was a very tasty dish. Mrs McGegan makes
the point that it is essential to cook slowly or the kidney
will get hard; she also says that any left-over peas or
beans can be added.

She makes this quantity for two meals for herself, as it
is perfectly good reheated.

Breast of Lamb Special

Sent by Miss P. Vernon of Southend-on-Sea, Essex.

Serves 3

Oven temperature:* 400°F, gas mark 6, lowered to
350° F, gas mark 4

Cooking time: approximately 1 hour 40 minutes

INGREDIENTS

1 breast of lamb	a little dried onion
1 heaped teaspoon rice	salt and pepper to taste
1 heaped teaspoon barley	1 packet of sage and onion
1 large potato, diced	stuffing
1 carrot, diced	

METHOD

1 Chop breast of lamb into portions and place in medium-sized baking tin.
2 Cook in the oven for 20 minutes, take out and pour off the fat.
3 Now add all the ingredients, except the stuffing, spreading them between the pieces of meat. Half cover with hot water and return to oven to simmer gently (covering the tin with foil) until well cooked.
4 Mix stuffing with hot water and spread over the dish.
5 Return to the oven (uncovered) to brown. Extra gravy can be made if required.

*Notes from test cooking. We cooked the breast of lamb for 20 minutes at 400°F, gas mark 6. The meat and vegetables were then simmered for a further hour (lowering the oven to 350°F, gas mark 4, once simmering point was reached). If necessary raise the temperature again to brown the stuffing. Together, allow approximately 1 hour 40 minutes for this dish.

Miss Vernon says that she devised this recipe during the war when she had a small café on the Isle of Wight. She was only allowed 1 pennyworth of meat per customer so had to be a bit of a magician to conjure up tasty meals; this was always a favourite.

Stuffed Breast of Lamb

Sent by Mr W. J. Smale of Tring, Hertfordshire.

Serves 2–3

Oven temperature: 350°F, gas mark 4

Cooking time: approximately 2 hours

INGREDIENTS

1 large breast of lamb, boned
half a packet of stuffing*
a small cabbage, shredded
1 or 2 carrots, cut small

1 or 2 potatoes, cut small (and
   any other vegetables if
   liked)
a small tin of pease pudding

   * You may like to try a lemon-flavoured stuffing.

METHOD

1   Cut off excess fat from the lamb (see note (a) below).
2   Stuff with the stuffing which has been mixed according to packet instructions. Roll and tie up with string.
3   Place in oven at 350°F, gas mark 4, for approximately 2 hours.
4   Meanwhile boil the vegetables and heat the pease pudding (see note (b) below).
5   Place cooked breast of lamb on kitchen paper and pat all over to remove surplus grease. Serve with gravy, if liked.

   Notes from test cooking. (a) If you go to a friendly butcher he may trim the joint for you. It is certainly necessary to cut off as much excess fat as possible, otherwise the result is too greasy.

(b) The contents of the tin of pease pudding can be heated in a fireproof dish in the oven for a short while to save using another burner on top of the stove.

Lemon Sponge Pudding

Sent by Mrs Sybil Watt of Bournemouth, Hampshire.

Serves 2–3

Oven temperature: 350°F, gas mark 4

Cooking time: 30–40 minutes

INGREDIENTS

1 oz. margarine
3 oz. caster sugar
1 lemon

1 oz. self-raising flour
1 egg, separated
quarter of a pint milk

METHOD

1 Cream the margarine and sugar.
2 Add the juice and grated rind of lemon.
3 Sieve in the flour and mix lightly.
4 Add the lightly beaten yolk of egg and beat well.
5 Add the milk and stir till blended.

6   Beat the egg white until stiff and fold it into the
    mixture.
7   Pour into a well greased ovenware dish and stand it in
    a deep tin containing hot water.
8   Bake in a moderate oven, 350°F, gas mark 4, for
    30–40 minutes. When ready this pudding has a
    sponge top and lemon-curd-like base. It should be
    served hot.

Notes from test cooking. This recipe is similar to a very
popular recipe which I gave in *Easy Cooking for One or Two*
but this one uses milk instead of water. In the method
above there may be some curdling when the liquid is
stirred in, but this does not affect the lightness of the
sponge.

As an alternative method of mixing, I found that if you
use soft margarine you can place all the ingredients,
except the egg white, in the mixing bowl and beat them
together till smooth, 2–3 minutes, then merely fold in the
beaten white.

We all wanted second helpings of Mrs Watt's Lemon
Sponge Pudding.

Liver and Stuffing

Sent by Mrs E. Harland of Reading, who wrote: 'I
enclose this recipe which I use for a one pan meal. Living
alone one is inclined to get lazy about cooking, though I

strongly support the fact that home cooked meals are more satisfying and help one to keep fit.'

Serves 2–3

Oven temperature: 350°F, gas mark 4

Cooking time: 1 hour 15 minutes

INGREDIENTS

half lb. ox liver
2 onions
2 oz. white breadcrumbs*
salt and pepper

1 tablespoon chopped parsley
half teaspoon mixed herbs
dash Worcestershire sauce
1 oz. dripping

Garnish with fresh tomatoes.

METHOD

1   Slice the liver (butcher may do this for you) and place in a greased ovenproof dish.
2   Peel and chop onions. Mix with breadcrumbs, salt, pepper, parsley, herbs and sauce.
3   Spread over the liver.
4   Dot with dripping and cover the dish tightly with lid or foil.
5   Bake at 350°F, gas mark 4, for 1 hour.
6   Remove the lid and bake for a further 15 minutes until tender.

Notes from test cooking. We found that this comfortably served three so it is good to serve for guests.

At step 2, we wondered why no fluid was added, but in

fact it was not necessary, enough gravy came out of the liver to make it nice and moist.

*We did not bother to grate the breadcrumbs but just coarsely broke up stale bread with the fingers.

Liver is particularly rich in iron, vitamins A and D and protein so this is a very nourishing dish as well as a tasty one.

Baked Omelette

Sent by Miss B. E. Smith of Croydon, Surrey.

Serves 1

Oven temperature: 350°F, gas mark 4

Cooking time: 30–35 minutes

INGREDIENTS

1 tomato
pepper and salt
chopped chives (or onion)
2 eggs
3 tablespoons milk

one and a half oz. grated
   cheese
1–2 tablespoons left-over
   cooked vegetables

METHOD

1 Grease an ovenproof dish, slice the tomato over the base and season.
2 Add some chopped chives.

3 Beat the eggs and milk together with seasoning.
4 Add the grated cheese and any left-over cooked vegetables (e.g. peas, or cut-up beans, carrots).
5 Pour into the dish and bake at 350°F, gas mark 4, for 30–35 minutes. Serve immediately.

Notes from test cooking. As we could not get chives we used a little, very finely chopped onion. The cooked vegetables gave an attractive appearance and this dish makes 2 eggs into a substantial meal.

Paprika Beef

Sent by Mr G. A. Parkinson of Sittingbourne, Kent (who also sent the recipe for Woolton Pie, page 197).

Serves 2

Oven temperature: 350°F, gas mark 4

Cooking time: approximately 1 hour 30 minutes

INGREDIENTS

2 slices of topside of beef (8 oz. the two)
seasoning
flour
half a teaspoon paprika
a little butter and oil for frying

2 medium onions, sliced
a little stock
tomato ketchup
Worcestershire sauce
thyme

Can be served with potatoes and carrots.

METHOD

1   Season the beef with salt and pepper. Now mix the
    flour and paprika and coat the meat with it.
2   Fry the meat in a mixture of butter and oil until
    golden.
3   Take meat out of pan and place in a casserole and
    then fry sliced onions until nicely coloured. Put the
    onions on top of the meat.
4   Swill out the pan with stock and a little tomato
    ketchup and 3 drops of Worcestershire sauce. Pour
    over the meat and sprinkle with a little thyme.
5   Cover the casserole and put into a medium hot oven.
    (If preferred, use a *flameproof* casserole or saucepan
    and cook on top of the stove instead of in the oven.) It
    should be tender in about 1 hour 30 minutes but test
    for tenderness after an hour or so.
6   This meal can be served with boiled potatoes and
    cooked sliced carrots.

Notes from test cooking. Although this was not a cheap
cut of beef it was very tender with no wastage.

Potato Pancakes

Sent by Gertrude Quick of Chingford, London E4.

Serves 2

INGREDIENTS

2 large potatoes   salt
1 large egg, beaten   oil for frying
1 tablespoon flour

METHOD

1   Grate 2 large raw peeled potatoes into a basin.
2   Strain off the fluid which collects.
3   Add to the grated potato the egg, flour and salt.
4   Fry in small pancakes until nice and crispy.

Notes from test cooking. Put in a heaped teaspoon of
mixture at a time. Allow plenty of time for frying these
pancakes so that the potato is well cooked through in the
shallow fat as well as browned on the outside.

Sausage and Mash Pie

Sent by Mrs A. Godwin of Ellesmere, Shropshire.
Serves 2 people; halve the recipe for 1 person
Oven temperature: 350°F, gas mark 4
Cooking time: approximately 35–40 minutes

INGREDIENTS

half a lb. pork sausage meat

1 large onion, chopped and
fried

1 apple, peeled, cored and
chopped

2 sliced tomatoes or canned
tomatoes

salt and pepper to taste

a little mashed potato

2 oz. grated cheese

METHOD

1   Cover the bottom of an ovenproof dish with sausage
meat.

2   Over this put the onion, fried soft but not brown, the
chopped apple and the sliced tomatoes, and season.

3   Cover with mashed potatoes, mixed with the grated
cheese.

4   Bake at 350°F, gas mark 4, for 35 minutes or longer,
until the sausage meat is well cooked and the top is
browned.

Notes from test cooking. For this recipe you can use either
left-over mashed potatoes or a small packet of reconstituted instant mashed potato.

6 to 1 Cake

Sent by Miss Doris Garcke of Leyton, E10. This is a
plain, everyday cake which is not too rich. It is an economical recipe as only 1 egg is required.

Oven temperature: 350°F, gas mark 4

Cooking time: approximately 1 hour

INGREDIENTS

6 oz. self-raising flour
5 oz. sugar
4 oz. margarine
3 tablespoons milk
2 oz. dried fruit
1 egg

You will need a cake tin 6–7 inches in diameter. Just grease well with margarine (there is no need to line the tin with greaseproof paper).

METHOD

1 Cream margarine and sugar together.
2 Beat egg well and add to the mixture together with the flour (sieved) and fruit and milk.
3 Mix well and turn into the greased tin.
4 Bake in a pre-heated oven at 350°F, gas mark 4, for approximately 1 hour.

Notes from test cooking. The margarine and sugar are sufficiently mixed when the mixture easily falls off the spoon into the bowl – give the spoon a sharp tap on the side of the mixing bowl. The cake is baked sufficiently when it is firm to the touch, browned on top and just beginning to shrink away from the sides of the tin.

Baked Suet Roll

Sent by Miss D. Eastwood of London, w1.

Serves 4, or 2 one day and (reheated) 2 the next

Oven temperature: 400°F, gas mark 6

Cooking time: 30 minutes (to reheat, use oven at 350°F, gas mark 4)

INGREDIENTS

three quarters of a lb. raw   8 oz. self-raising flour
  minced beef (*or* cooked   4–6 oz. shredded suet
  chicken *or* cold cooked meat)   fat or dripping for baking
1 packet or can oxtail soup

METHOD

1   Simmer the minced beef in the canned soup for about
    15 minutes. It may be necessary to add a little
    seasoning. *Or* simmer the minced beef in a cupful
    of water for 5 minutes; sprinkle in the packet oxtail
    soup and continue simmering for another 10 minutes.
    (Already cooked chicken or meat need only simmer
    for 5–10 minutes.)
2   Remove from the stove, drain all the liquid off into a
    small pan and leave the meat to cool.
3   Make crust with flour and suet, mix with a little
    water and roll out to an oblong. (For Suet Crust
    Pastry, see page 145.) Place drained meat in centre,

roll up and seal (dampen the edges of the suet pastry with water so that the roll seals to stop the filling from leaking out).

4   Place roll in tin with hot fat or dripping. To make the crust shine you can paint over with the yolk of an egg.

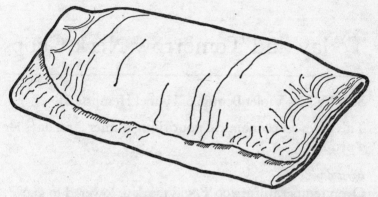

5   Bake for 30 minutes, but remember to baste with the fat two or three times.
6   With the liquid you can make a sauce and can add sherry or a little wine, which makes it delicious.

Notes from test cooking. We found this sufficient for four. Miss Eastwood said that it could be made for one day and heated up for the next day and we did this, making two meals for two people.

At step 1, because the oxtail soup is very strong in flavour it needs very little seasoning. At step 2 you may find that to drain the liquid from the meat is a little tricky unless you tip the meat into a sieve and let the liquor drain through.

At step 4 we felt it extravagant to use the yolk of an egg so we painted the crust over with a little milk; although this does not make it shine, it makes a pleasant golden colour.

Today and Tomorrow Neck Chops

Sent by Mrs Violet Benton of Hemel Hempstead.

This gives an economical nourishing dinner for 2 days for 2 people

First day
Oven temperature: 400°F, gas mark 6, lowered to 250°F, gas mark 1

Cooking time: approximately 2 hours 30 minutes

INGREDIENTS

1 pint home-made chicken stock plus 1 Oxo cube

or

1 pint water plus 2 Chicken Oxo cubes

3 middle-neck lamb chops (1 lb.)
1 small can carrots
half an onion, finely chopped, or a good pinch dried onion
1 teaspoon Worcestershire sauce (optional)

Serve with green vegetables and potatoes.

METHOD

1   Boil stock or water and crumble Oxo in it.
2   Put chops at the bottom of an ovenproof dish.
3   Add half of the tin of small carrots, together with the onion.
4   Pour stock and Worcestershire sauce over and cover the dish.
5   Cook for 2 hours 30 minutes in the oven, lowering the heat to 250°F, gas mark 1, when it simmers.
6   Serve 1 chop each with the carrots, gravy stock, mashed potatoes and seasonal vegetables.

Keep unused stock refrigerated or very cold for next day.

Next day

Oven temperature: 400°F, gas mark 6, lowered to 250°F, gas mark 1

Cooking time: approximately 2 hours

Take the remaining chop, cut all the meat off the bone and cut into small pieces; you will be surprised how much meat you will get.

EXTRA INGREDIENTS

3 heaped dessertspoons self-raising flour
pinch salt

three quarters of an oz. margarine

METHOD

1 Mix the flour, salt and margarine and rub together
  finely with the finger tips. Mix to a stiff pastry with a
  little water.
2 Roll out, onto a floured board, a round a size smaller
  than the top of your casserole.
3 Place the cut-up meat at the bottom of the casserole,
  add the remaining carrots from the day before and
  put the round of pastry on top.
4 Have the stock from the day before boiling, and pour
  over, making sure the pastry is covered.
5 Cover the casserole and put into the oven for 2 hours,
  beginning at 400°F, gas mark 6, but turn the heat
  down to 250°F, gas mark 1, as soon as the gravy
  boils.
6 Serve with vegetables.

Notes from test cooking. This recipe is certainly economical and tasty but you have to be prepared to spend
time and trouble on its preparation.

We recommend that the fat which solidifies by the
second day should be taken off before the stock is reheated.

The flavour was outstandingly good and we had
enough stock left over to make a delicious cupful of
soup.

Simple Welsh Rarebit

Sent by Dorothy Nicholson on behalf of her mother, Mrs Olive Margaret Nicholson of Sutton, Norwich.

Serves 1

INGREDIENTS

2 slices of toast
1 oz. margarine
1–2 teaspoons cornflour

half a small teacup milk
half a small teacup grated cheese

METHOD

1 Make the toast.
2 Melt the margarine in a saucepan.
3 Stir in the cornflour.
4 Add the milk and grated cheese and stir over gentle heat till smooth.
5 Spread over slices of toast.
6 Optional: Heat under the grill until light golden brown.

Notes from test cooking. We found this very good and simple, smooth not tough. Mrs Nicholson uses only 1 teaspoon of cornflour but we found 2 teaspoons necessary for thickening. That is because sizes of cups and spoons vary from one household to another.

RECIPES FROM QUEEN MARGARET COLLEGE STUDENTS

All-Bran Fruit Brack

This is similar to a recipe sent by Mrs E. Harris of Harlow, Essex. The high fibre All-bran and other amendments were made by the students of Queen Margaret College.

Oven temperature: 350°F, gas mark 4

Cooking time: 1 hour to 1 hour 15 minutes, depending on the shape of the tin (the best tin to use is a small loaf tin, greased)

INGREDIENTS

quarter of a pint warm
   strained tea
half a lb. mixed dried fruit
3 oz. brown sugar
one and a half oz. All-bran

one and half level tablespoons
   golden syrup
1 egg
6 oz. self-raising flour

METHOD

First day

1   Pour the warm strained tea over the fruit, sugar, All-bran and golden syrup in a mixing bowl. Stir, cover and leave overnight.

Second day

2 Beat the tea-soaked ingredients with the egg (no need to beat it separately first) and flour, until the mixture is of a dropping consistency (see Glossary, page 235).

3 Transfer to the tin, which you have greased well with margarine or lard.

4 Bake at 350°F, gas mark 4, until it is firm and beginning to shrink away from the sides of the tin. Test the cake with a skewer or knife (see Glossary).

5 Cool on a wire rack. It will keep well for a week or longer if wrapped in kitchen foil.

To serve, slice thinly and spread with butter or margarine.

Apple Anna

Serves 2

INGREDIENTS

1 oz. margarine
2 cooking apples

2–3 tablespoons brown or
   white sugar
1 banana

METHOD

1 Melt the margarine in a small saucepan.
2 Peel, core and slice apples.
3 Place in pan and sprinkle with the sugar.

4   Peel and slice the banana over the top of the apples.
5   Cover the pan and stew very gently stirring occasion-
    ally, until the apples are soft (10–12 minutes).
6   Optional: Serve hot with custard or top of the milk.

Apple and Lemon Crisp

Serves 2

INGREDIENTS

1 cooking apple, peeled and   juice of half a lemon
  cored   2 oz. digestive biscuits
1 level tablespoon sugar, or to   1 oz. margarine, melted
  taste

METHOD

1   Stew the apple in very little water. Sweeten.
2   Stir in the lemon juice. Pour into a serving dish and
    leave to cool.
3   Crush the biscuits to crumbs and mix with the melted
    margarine.
4   Sprinkle the biscuit mixture over the apple. Serve
    cold.

Store-cupboard alternative

Rhubarb Crisp

1 Use canned fruit, e.g. rhubarb. No need to cook, just drain off excess juice.
2 Top with biscuit mixture as above.

Curry Quickie

Serves 2

INGREDIENTS

2 rashers streaky bacon
1 teaspoon dried onion
1 small can curried beans

1 apple, grated
2 hard-boiled eggs (see page 16 for method)

METHOD

1 Trim and chop rashers and fry in a small saucepan till they start to become crisp.
2 Add onion and stir for a few moments with the bacon. Drain off excess fat.
3 Add beans and apple. Heat gently, stirring occasionally.
4 Shell eggs, quarter and serve with the curry.

Lentil Soup

Serves 2–3

INGREDIENTS

2 oz. lentils
1 pint water
1 carrot
1 small onion

1 rasher bacon
seasoning
quarter of a teaspoon curry
      powder (optional)

METHOD

1 Wash lentils and put to boil in 1 pint water.
2 Cut carrot, onion and bacon very small and add to
   lentils.
3 Season, adding curry powder if liked.
4 Simmer gently for 1 hour, or until lentils are soft.

Quick Pea Soup

Serves 2

INGREDIENTS

1 small potato
1 chicken stock cube
half a pint hot water

1 small can garden peas
salt and pepper (optional)

METHOD

1 Peel and dice the potato.

2 Put in saucepan with chicken stock cube dissolved in half a pint of hot water.
3 Bring to the boil, stirring. Cover and simmer for about 10 minutes.
4 Stir in the peas, with their liquid, and reheat. Taste for seasoning.
5 Optional: If you like a purée soup you can sieve, stir well and reheat before serving.

Skirlie (Skirl-in-the-pan)

Serves 2

INGREDIENTS

1 onion, finely chopped
1 oz. margarine, lard, dripping or suet

2–3 oz. oatmeal
salt and pepper

METHOD

1 In a frying pan, fry the onion till lightly browned in the hot fat.
2 Add the oatmeal and fry gently to absorb the fat for 5–10 minutes till thoroughly cooked.
3 Season and serve with green vegetables, e.g. cabbage.

Skirlie can be a substitute for either potatoes or meat in a meal.

Stovies

Serves 2–3. Serve with cold meat, or sausages, bacon or ham.

INGREDIENTS

1 oz. dripping or lard   salt
1 small onion, peeled   water
1 lb. potatoes, peeled

You will need a medium-sized saucepan.

METHOD

1 Melt the dripping or lard
2 Stir in the thinly sliced onion.
3 Add the potatoes, peeled and cut in thick slices or chunks.
4 Season with salt.
5 Pour in only just enough water to cover the bottom of the pan, to prevent burning.
6 Cover tightly and cook on a low heat 20–30 minutes till soft, stirring occasionally.

Chapter 3
Simple Cooking

I have had several letters from people who say they are cutting down on cooking because of the cost of fuel. But do you realize how little you spend on fuel compared to the cost of the food?

- A Sunday lunch for two – say half a shoulder of lamb, roast potatoes, carrots, apple pie – all cooked in the oven, could cost in fuel less than the price of a couple of the carrots or one of the apples.
- Even the prolonged boiling of 6 lb. of marmalade costs less than the price of one of the oranges.

Going without enjoyable hot meals is false economy. Far better to use the fuel to best advantage.

There are several ways to do this:

(a) Use the equipment especially designed for the job, e.g.:

an *electric toaster* is cheaper on fuel than the grill for toast,

an *electric kettle* is the most economical way of boiling water, a *pressure cooker* saves a considerable amount of fuel on the long-cooking dishes such as casseroles.

However, if you do not already possess such an item it would be foolish to advise you to buy one in order to save fuel – it would take you ages to recoup in fuel-saving the cost of the equipment. Let's hope you get one as a gift!

(b) Use the preheating time of the oven, unless you are cooking items such as scones or sponge cakes which need short sharp cooking. It is a waste to heat up an empty oven – the heating-up time is the period in which most fuel is consumed.

(c) Probably the most satisfactory way of seeing that you are saving fuel is to cook several dishes in the oven together.

Suggestions:

Menu No. 1

Baked Omelette
Honeyed Apples

Menu No. 2

Baked Fish
Lemon Sponge Pudding

Menu No. 3

Savoury Egg Custard
Rhubarb and Orange (or
    Apple) Crumble

Menu No. 4

Hot Sardine and Tomato
Banana Pinwheels

Menu No. 5

Beef and Tatie Pie *or* Fish
    Crumble with Sauce
Baked Apples

Menu No. 6

Frankfurter Bake
Spicy Rice Pudding

Menu No. 7
Cheese Soufflé
Osborne Pudding

Note: Serve a cut-up raw tomato with the Cheese Soufflé, otherwise this meal might look a monotonous ye llow.

Other ideas for making full use of your oven:
(1) While you are cooking Scone Pizza or Bacon and Kidney Toad-in-the-Hole for yourself, you could cook a Mincemeat Plait or an Easter Ring if you are expecting guests later in the day.
(2) If you are making an Easy-Mix Christmas Cake or Easy-Mix Simnel Cake you could cook at the same time an easy lunch dish: Frankfurter Bake.
(3) Stuffed Lamb's Heart takes 2 hours of oven space, but at the same time you could use the oven for baking an Ovaltine Fruit Loaf and/or an Apple and Ginger Upside-Down Cake.
(4) While the oven is on at 350°F, gas mark 4, you could cook a 6 to 1 Cake or an All-bran Fruit Brack.

Other dishes which take an hour or more of oven space at 350°F are: Lamb Parcel; Liver and Stuffing; Love-Apple Lamb; Meat Loaf; Paprika Beef; Chicken and Orange Casserole; Woolton Pie; Beef Layer Pie – so any of these could be cooked at the same time as one of the cakes.

But if you are feeling lazy while you are cooking the

cakes, you could just pop into the oven a 'quickie' Egg Nest for a snack.

But I stress again that the cost of fuel for cooking is only a fraction of that spent on the food; so do not have a guilt feeling if you are too tired to prepare several dishes for cooking together.

Apple Charlotte

(one of the favourites of a seventy-seven-year-old enthusiastic cook)

Serves 2

Oven temperature: 325°F, gas mark 3

Cooking time: 90 minutes

INGREDIENTS

a little butter and granulated sugar

3–4 oz. left-over bread and butter

or

stale bread

or

stale cake

1 cooking apple

2 oz. butter or margarine

3 tablespoons sugar (brown if possible)

rind and juice of 1 lemon

ground cinnamon (optional)

METHOD

1 Butter an ovenproof dish and shake in a little granulated sugar to stick to the butter and coat the dish.

2 Crumble or coarsely grate the bread or cake into a basin.

3 Peel and grate the apple and add to the bread or cake.

4 Melt the 2 oz. butter or margarine with the 3 table-spoons sugar in a small pan. Add the lemon. Pour into the basin.

5 Thoroughly mix the ingredients together, adding ground cinnamon if liked.

6 Turn into the prepared ovenproof dish.

7 Bake at 325°F, gas mark 3, for 90 minutes.

Serve hot or cold with ice cream, whipped cream, custard or top of the milk.

Bacon and Kidney Toad-in-the-Hole

Serves 2

Oven temperature: 425°F, gas mark 7

Cooking time: 25 minutes

INGREDIENTS

4 oz. cooked bacon
1 lamb's kidney

1 tomato
a knob of lard

Batter

1 oz. plain flour   2 tablespoons milk
pinch of salt   1 tablespoon water
1 standard egg

METHOD

1 To make the batter, sift the flour and salt into a bowl,
   make a well in the centre and drop in the egg (unbeaten).

2 Add a tablespoon of the milk and begin to mix
   smoothly with a wooden spoon.

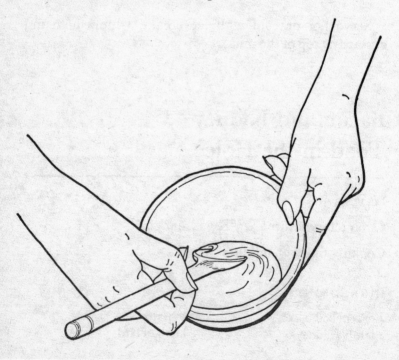

3 Add the tablespoon of water to make a thick batter and beat till full of air bubbles and the spoon makes a 'plopping' sound.
4 Stir in the remaining tablespoon of milk taking care not to expel air.

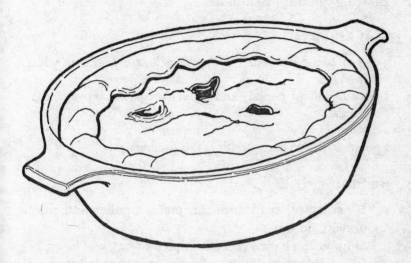

5 Cut the cooked bacon and the raw kidney into small pieces. Cut the tomato into quarters or eighths.
6 Melt the lard in an ovenproof dish and, when it is hot, pour in the batter. Add the bacon, kidney and tomato.
7 Bake at 425°F, gas mark 7, for 25 minutes, until light, well-risen and golden.

Bacon Pieces and Cabbage

Serves 2

Cooking time: 15–20 minutes

INGREDIENTS

3 or 4 oz. bacon pieces or trimmings

1 small onion, peeled and halved

1 bay leaf

2 potatoes, peeled and halved

half a lb. (or less) firm white salad cabbage

half a teaspoon caraway seeds (optional)

pepper

salt (optional)

METHOD

1   If necessary, cut the bacon pieces smaller and rinse under cold water.

2   Simmer the bacon pieces, onion and bay leaf in water for a few minutes (skim, if necessary, once it has come to the boil).

3   Add the potatoes and simmer for about 5 minutes.

4   Add the cabbage, cut into medium shreds, and the caraway seeds. Simmer for a further 5–10 minutes, till the cabbage and potatoes feel tender when prodded with a sharp knife.

5   Drain carefully to retain as many caraway seeds as possible. Taste for seasoning – you will probably want to add pepper, but may not need salt. Remove the bay leaf before serving.

Baked Beans and Sausages

Serves 2 – halve quantities for 1

INGREDIENTS

4 oz. sausages
fat for frying
2 tablespoons onion, finely
  chopped
16-oz. can baked beans in
  tomato sauce

1 tablespoon wine vinegar
1–2 tablespoons demerara
  sugar
1 level teaspoon made English
  mustard

METHOD

1 Fry the sausages gently in a saucepan, using very little fat for frying. When the sausages are thoroughly cooked remove from the pan and cut in pieces.
2 In the same fat, fry the onion until well softened. Drain off any surplus fat.
3 Add the baked beans to the onion with the vinegar, sugar, mustard and cooked sausages and heat until the flavours are well blended.

Notes from test cooking. This was based on a *Good Housekeeping* recipe, but as that used the oven I tried this alternative for those of you who prefer top-of-the-stove cooking. In the original recipe there is no need to fry the onions or cook the sausages first – the slit sausages (thick ones, not chipolatas) are merely placed on top of the other ingredients and baked at 350°F, gas mark 4, for 45 minutes.

Baked Fish

Serves 2

Oven temperature: 350°F, gas mark 4

Cooking time: approximately 40 minutes

INGREDIENTS

1 small onion, thinly sliced
half a lb. fillet of white fish
salt and pepper
lemon juice

2 medium-sized tomatoes,
  skinned and sliced
1 tablespoon grated cheese
1 tablespoon packet stuffing

METHOD

1 Grease a shallow ovenproof dish and then arrange the thinly sliced onion over the bottom of the dish.
2 Trim and wash the fish, cut in two and place on top of the onion.
3 Season with salt, pepper and lemon juice.
4 Cover fish with sliced tomatoes.
5 Mix cheese and dry stuffing and sprinkle over the top.
6 Bake, covered, in oven at 350°F, gas mark 4, for approximately 30 minutes, remove lid or foil and bake uncovered for a further 10 minutes.

Note from test cooking. This brings back memories – it is almost identical to the first recipe I ever broadcast, on Woman's Hour in 1952!

Beefburgers with Barbecue Sauce

Serves 1 or more. According to appetite, allow 1 or 2 beefburgers per person. This amount of sauce is sufficient to baste 6 beefburgers, so, if you are making fewer, you can cut down slightly on the sauce ingredients.

INGREDIENTS

2 oz. minced beef for each   salt
   beefburger   pepper
a little onion, finely diced

Sauce

1 small onion, diced   1 teaspoon Worcestershire
half an oz. margarine   sauce
2 tablespoons tomato ketchup   quarter of a pint water
1 dessertspoon vinegar   salt and pepper

METHOD

1 Simmer all the sauce ingredients in a small saucepan for 10 minutes.
2 With a fork mix together beef, onion and seasoning. Shape into beefburgers.
3 Cook the beefburgers for approximately 20 minutes in

the sauce, with frequent basting. Either use a hot oven (375°F, gas mark 5) or cook (turning) under a medium grill. Make sure they are cooked and hot right through to the centre.

Beef and Tatie Pie

Serves 2

Oven temperature: 400°F, gas mark 6

Cooking time: 20 minutes on top of stove, followed by approximately 20–30 minutes in oven

INGREDIENTS

1 oz. dripping or lard
4 oz. raw minced beef
half pint stock (can be made with water and stock cube)
1 small onion
1 large potato
1 teaspoon gravy mix or cornflour

pinch mixed herbs
salt and pepper (if needed)
6–8 oz. ready-mix shortcrust pastry
or
shortcrust pastry using 4 oz. flour and 2 oz. fat (see p. 143)
a little milk

METHOD

1   Melt lard in pan, add minced beef and cook for a few minutes, stirring.
2   Add stock, place lid on pan and simmer 10 minutes.

3 Add chopped onion, cook for 5 minutes.
4 Peel and dice potato, add to pan, cook for 5 minutes.
5 Blend gravy mix or cornflour with a little water and add to pan.
6 Add mixed herbs and stir well; bring to the boil, stirring, and taste for seasoning.
7 Using a straining spoon or similar, place meat mixture in pie dish with a little gravy (serve remainder of gravy separately).
8 Cover with shortcrust pastry, brush with milk, and cook at 400°F, gas mark 6, till cooked and beginning to colour (approximately 20–30 minutes).

Carrot Salad

INGREDIENTS

fresh carrots   a few currants, washed
1 lemon

METHOD

1 Peel the carrots and grate coarsely.
2 Moisten well with lemon juice.
3 Stir in some currants – their sweetness takes off a little of the sharpness of the lemon.

Casserole of Chicken

Serves 1 or 2

Oven temperature: 400°F, gas mark 6

Cooking time: approximately 1 hour 30 minutes

INGREDIENTS

knob of butter or margarine
1 large potato, very thinly
    sliced
1 small onion, very thinly
    sliced
pepper and salt

1 tablespoon packet stuffing
1 tomato (optional)
1 or 2 slices bacon
1 or 2 chicken joints
pinch of thyme
2 tablespoons water or stock

METHOD

1   Grease a casserole dish well with butter or margarine,
    place potato very thinly sliced on the base of the dish
    with a layer of onions and then potato, seasoning each
    layer.
2   Mix stuffing with a little water or stock (as directed
    on packet) to form the next layer and place on top
    with the sliced tomato, if used.
3   Wrap the de-rinded bacon round the chicken joints.
    Place on top of the casserole, sprinkling on thyme and
    moistening with the 2 tablespoons of water or stock.
4   Cover and cook for 1 hour with the lid on. Remove
    the lid and cook a further 30 minutes to brown the
    chicken.

Comment from test cooking. Delicious and very substantial. The chicken was well done and crisp. We ate it with cauliflower but dressed salad would have been nice too.

Cauliflower Cheese

Serves 2 – halve quantities for 1

INGREDIENTS

1 small cauliflower
half a pint of one-stage cheese
  sauce (see page 129)

a little extra grated cheese
  (optional)

METHOD

1 Cut the cauliflower into sprigs, and also cut up the tender green leaves.
2 Boil in salted water till tender (about 7–10 minutes – test for 'doneness' with a sharp pointed knife). Drain.
3 Meanwhile make the sauce.
4 Arrange the cauliflower in a heatproof dish and pour the sauce over. If you like, sprinkle with a little extra grated cheese and heat under a hot grill till the surface bubbles and begins to brown.

Store-cupboard alternative. Use frozen broccoli and packet cheese sauce, made up thick.

Cheese and Haddock Puff

Serves 2

Oven temperature: 350°F, gas mark 4

Cooking time: approximately 30–35 minutes

INGREDIENTS

2 thin slices white bread (from small loaf)

2 oz. Cheddar cheese, sliced

4 oz. smoked haddock or smoked cod fillet (skinned and cut into small pieces*)

1 egg

quarter of a pint milk

a shake of pepper

* Use a very sharp knife or scissors – or ask the fishmonger to do this for you.

To serve: grilled tomatoes (optional).

METHOD

1   Remove crusts and cut bread into fingers. Arrange in alternate layers with cheese and haddock in a half- or three-quarter-pint ovenproof dish.

2   Beat egg lightly, add milk and pepper.

3   Pour over ingredients in dish.

4   Bake at 350°F, gas mark 4, for about 30–35 minutes. Remove lid or cover about 10 minutes before the end of cooking time.

5   Serve with grilled tomatoes, if liked.

Chicken (or Turkey) in Mustard-Cheese Sauce

This recipe is economical because it makes a little cold cooked chicken or turkey go a long way. It is still a good protein meal because of the additional milk and cheese.

Serves 2 or 3

Oven temperature: 400°F, gas mark 6

Cooking time in oven: 20 minutes

INGREDIENTS

a little cold, cooked chicken or turkey (about enough for 1
    serving)
2 sausages, cooked,
or
some left-over sausage-meat stuffing
vegetables, e.g. tomato, sweetcorn, peas or mixed vegetables
    (cooked if necessary, e.g. if a packet of frozen vegetables is
    used)
half a pint thick cheese sauce (see step 2 below)
1 rounded dessertspoon *French* mustard

METHOD

1   Cut up poultry and sausage and put with vegetables
    in a pie dish or casserole.
2   Make a thick cheese sauce (see page 129 for one-stage
    method).

3　Stir the French mustard into the sauce – use plenty to make it well-flavoured.

4　Pour the sauce over the top of the poultry, sausage and vegetables.

5　Bake, uncovered, at 400°F, gas mark 6, for about 20 minutes.

Chop, Chicken or Fish in Foil

Serves 1

Oven temperature: 375°F, gas mark 5

Cooking time: 30–45 minutes

INGREDIENTS

1 small onion

knob of butter or margarine

1 pork or lamb chop or chicken portion or fish cutlet per person

a few mushrooms, sliced

salt and pepper

1 tablespoon plain yogurt per portion

Serve with carrots, greens or tomatoes.

You will need kitchen foil.

METHOD

1　Peel and slice the onion and fry it gently in the fat until softened and slightly golden.

2　Trim fat if necessary and put chop, chicken or fish

(washed and patted dry) in the centre of a square of kitchen foil.

3 Add raw mushrooms, fried onions, seasoning and yogurt.

4 Fold over the foil to make a loose packet.

5 Bake in moderate oven, 375°F, gas mark 5, for 30–45 minutes or till tender (fish will not take as long as meat).

6 Open the foil carefully to avoid steam, and turn the contents, with the juices, on to the plate. You will find that the yogurt may curdle slightly but this will not affect the flavour. To add colour to the plate, serve with cooked carrots or greens or with a raw or baked tomato.

Cidered Herring (Summer)

Serves 2

Oven temperature: 275°F, gas mark 1

Cooking time: 1 hour – then leave it to get cold

INGREDIENTS

2 fresh herrings (cleaned, and heads and fins removed)

quarter to half a pint of cider

Sauce

1 small orange
1 carton plain yogurt

watercress or salad cress

METHOD

1   Place the prepared herrings in an ovenproof dish.
2   Pour over the cider and bake in a slow oven, 275°F, gas mark 1, for 1 hour.
3   Remove from the oven and leave to cool for at least 2 hours in the liquid.
4   To make the sauce: Cut the orange in half and spoon out the segments (without pith) into the yogurt. Snip in plenty of watercress or salad cress (sometimes sold as 'mustard and cress' or 'growing cress').
5   Put the cidered herrings on to the plates. Pour the yogurt sauce over.

Cidered Herring (Winter)

Serves 2

Oven temperature: 375°F, gas mark 5

Cooking time: approximately 45 minutes

INGREDIENTS

1 medium onion
2 small red eating apples
half a pint of cider
1 chicken-stock cube crumbled into the cider
half a teaspoon salt

shake of pepper
2 fresh herrings (cleaned and boned by the fishmonger)
1 teaspoon cornflour blended with 1 tablespoon water

METHOD

1 Peel the onion and cut into quarter-inch-thick rings. Core the apples (do not peel) and cut into quarter-inch-thick slices or rings.

2 Mix the onion and apple together and place in the bottom of an ovenproof dish.

3 Pour over the cider and stock mixture.

4 Season. Cover the dish with foil or lid and bake at 375°F, gas mark 5.

5 After 20 minutes, remove the dish from the oven, uncover and place the herrings on top. Re-cover and bake for a further 20–25 minutes.

6 Lift the apples, onions and herrings on to a serving dish or straight on to the plates. Keep warm.

7 Thicken the cidery liquid with cornflour (see 'Blend' – Glossary, page 234). Pour over the herrings and serve immediately.

Colcannon

Serves 2 good portions

INGREDIENTS

half a lb. potatoes
half a lb. cabbage

1 oz. butter or dripping
salt and pepper

METHOD (using one pot)

1 Boil peeled and cut-up potatoes till half cooked (approximately 5 minutes).
2 Cut the washed cabbage in medium shreds and add to the pan. Bring back to the boil and simmer till potatoes and cabbage are tender when pierced with a sharp knife.
3 Tip out into a colander to drain off all the water.
4 Melt butter or dripping in the saucepan.
5 Add the potatoes and mash well, then chop in the cabbage. Season to taste and mix well until it is thoroughly hot.
6 OPTIONAL If you want, the mixture can be turned into a greased pie dish, sprinkled with grated cheese, dotted with small pieces of butter or margarine and browned under the grill or in a hot oven.

Bubble and Squeak

This is similar in ingredients to Colcannon, but the flavour is different because it uses left-over, not freshly cooked, vegetables; they are then fried and browned.

INGREDIENTS

left-over mashed potatoes
left-over cooked cabbage, chopped

salt and pepper
butter

METHOD

1 Mix the potatoes and cabbage, with seasoning to taste.
2 Heat some butter in a frying pan and mash the vegetables and flatten them down smoothly.
3 Fry until the mixture is browned underneath, then, if possible, turn it over with a palette knife or slice to brown the other side and heat it all thoroughly.

Good served with cold meat and pickles.

Courgettes

Courgettes look and taste like baby marrows, but they are only related: a small courgette will never grow into a marrow. They are useful vegetables for small-scale cooking because you can buy one or two at a time.

Serves 1

Cooking time: 10–15 minutes

INGREDIENTS

1 or 2 small courgettes
a large knob of butter
salt and pepper

1 tomato, peeled and sliced (optional)

METHOD

1 Wash the courgettes but do not peel. Merely cut off

the two tips then slice fairly thinly (about a quarter of
an inch or less).

2   Melt the butter in a small saucepan, add the sliced
courgettes and tomato, if used, season with salt and
pepper.

3   Cover the pan and cook over gentle heat, shaking the
pan occasionally to prevent burning. The courgettes
should be tender in 10–15 minutes.

Creamy Onion Soup

This recipe was sent to me by another 'Louise Davies',
who is an S.R.N., S.C.M. It seems we also share an
interest in cooking! She writes: 'I make onion soup for
an old lady of eighty-three. She loves it, so does her niece
when she visits her aunt.'

Serves 1 large helping, or 2 smaller

INGREDIENTS

1 large onion
1 tablespoon sunflower seed oil
or
half an oz. margarine
1 dessertspoon flour
half a pint milk (or
  reconstituted dried
  skimmed)

pepper
celery salt
chopped parsley
good pinch of marjoram
half a chicken stock cube

METHOD

1 Peel and finely chop onion.
2 Melt margarine or heat oil in pan.
3 Add onion and sweat (see Glossary, page 243) over low heat for 5 minutes, stirring all the time.
4 Add flour and mix well with onion and fat – cook for a minute or two.
5 Off the heat, add milk slowly, stirring continuously to avoid lumps.
6 Return to heat, add seasonings, herbs and stock cube.
7 Cover and simmer over low heat, stirring occasionally, until the onion is soft.

Dumplings

Serves 2

INGREDIENTS

2 oz. self-raising flour
pinch of salt
shake of pepper

1 oz. shredded suet
cold water to mix

METHOD

1 Mix all dry ingredients with enough cold water to make a firm dough.
2 Flour the hands, roll dough into two large or four smaller balls.

3 Put into soup or stew and simmer gently for 15–20
   minutes with the lid on the saucepan.

If you prefer brown dumplings on top of a baked
casserole, do not replace the lid after the dumplings are
put in and cook near the top of the oven for 20 minutes at
400°F, gas mark 6.

Store-cupboard note. The basic dumplings and herb
dumplings can be store-cupboard recipes; the other
variations given below call for some fresh ingredients.

Flavoured dumplings:

Bacon Dumplings

Add a rasher of crisp bacon, cut into small pieces, 1
tablespoon chopped parsley and 1 dessertspoon tomato
ketchup.

Herb Dumplings

Add half a level teaspoon mixed dried herbs or 1 teaspoon
chopped fresh herbs.

Sausage Meat Dumplings

Add 2 oz. sausage meat and a quarter of a teaspoon dried
sage to basic mixture.

Mushroom Dumplings

Add 1 oz. finely chopped mushrooms (soften first in a little butter).

Lemon and Thyme Dumplings

Add the grated rind of about a quarter of a lemon and a quarter of a teaspoon dried thyme to the dry ingredients.

Grilled Herring

Serves 1

Total grilling time: approximately 15–20 minutes

INGREDIENTS

1 fresh herring, cleaned and boned

salt

black pepper

dried thyme

fresh lemon juice

Serve with brown bread and butter.

METHOD

1 Turn the boned herring flesh side upwards, removing any large loose bones, sprinkle with salt and black pepper and lightly with dried thyme.
2 Close up the herring and grill until the skin blisters (no butter or other fat required). Turn and grill the other side.

3 Open up carefully and grill the inside till cooked but
   NOT overcooked (this is the secret to retain the flavour).
4 Serve with plenty of fresh lemon juice and brown
   bread and butter.

Comment from Mr W. B. Sutton, who sent me this
recipe: I think this is superior to grilled trout.

Note on boning herring. Ask the fishmonger to clean the
fish and remove the centre bone – he can do this swiftly
and easily. If you have to do it yourself: Cut off the head,
scrape off the scales, slit to remove the interior but keep
the roes, if any, for frying and serving on toast for another
meal. Turn skin side upwards and run your fingers and
thumb along the spine, pressing until the bone is free.
This can, with a little practice, be removed in one piece
complete with tail.

Honeyed Apples

Serves 2

Oven temperature: 350–375°F, gas mark 4–5

Cooking time: 30 minutes

INGREDIENTS

1 large or 2 small cooking   1–2 tablespoons clear honey
  apples

METHOD

1   Peel, quarter and core the apples. Cut into slices a
    quarter to half an inch thick.
2   Place in a fairly deep, ovenproof dish.
3   Trickle the honey over the apples.
4   Bake in oven 350–375°F, gas mark 4–5, for about 30
    minutes, basting once or turning the apples over into
    the honey and oozing juice if you think they look dry.
    At the end of the cooking time they should be soft and
    light golden.
5   Serve hot or cold, either on their own or with any milk
    pudding, cream or top of the milk.

Kidney Jacket Potatoes

Serves 1

INGREDIENTS

1 potato baked in its jacket   salt and pepper
    (see recipe, page 23)   squeeze of lemon juice
1 lamb's kidney   optional additions: a little
half an onion (or 1 very small   left-over cooked lamb;
    onion)   streaky bacon, diced; a few
fat for frying   mushrooms

Can be served with a green vegetable, e.g. spring greens.

METHOD

1 Bake the potato in its jacket (see page 23).
2 With a sharp knife, chop up the kidney into several pieces, removing skin and the tough middle part, and chop up the onion.
3 Using a small frying pan fry the cut-up onion till soft. Add the kidney and fry for a few minutes more till just cooked. If you are adding cut-up lamb, bacon or mushrooms, fry them with the onion and kidney.
4 Season well and add a squeeze of lemon juice.
5 Cut the potato in two halves, remove the soft part inside and quickly mash with the kidney mixture, including the gravy which has come from the cooking.
6 Pile back into the potato cases and serve hot.

Lamb Parcel

Serves 2–3 (can be served cold next day)
Oven temperature: 350°F, gas mark 4
Cooking time: 40 minutes per lb.

INGREDIENTS

1 lean breast of lamb, boned   packet sage-and-onion or
1–2 tablespoons pickle   parsley-and-thyme stuffing

Can be served with roast potatoes and a green vegetable.

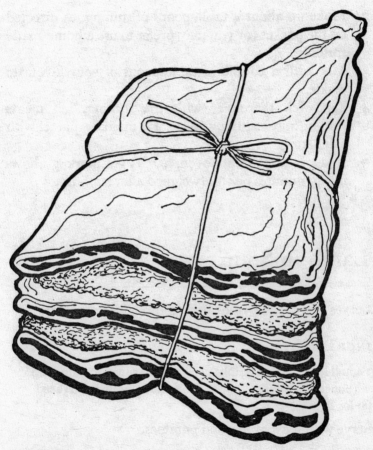

METHOD

1   Although it is possible to bone a breast of lamb with a
     sharp knife, most butchers will do this for you if you
     give due notice or shop at a slack period. Trim off
     excess fat, and cut the breast into three equal-sized,
     more or less square pieces.

2   Make up about 4 tablespoons of stuffing, as directed
    on the packet (or you may prefer to use a home-made
    stuffing).
3   Mix with a couple of tablespoons of your favourite
    pickle.
4   Sandwich the meat with the stuffing, i.e. meat:
    stuffing:meat:stuffing:meat. Tie up like a parcel with
    thin string.
5   Roast in a moderate oven, 350°F, gas mark 4, allow-
    ing 40 minutes per lb. (weighed after stuffing).

Lamb in Soup

Serves 2–3. Can be re-heated (thoroughly) next day.

INGREDIENTS

1 small lean breast of lamb   1 small can of tomato soup
   (boned if possible)   1 onion, peeled and sliced
fat for frying

Serve with toast or mashed potatoes.

METHOD

1   Cut the trimmed breast of lamb into 1-inch squares
    (see *Notes from test cooking*, below)
2   In a saucepan, fry the squares of meat till crisp.
    Drain.

3   Add the contents of the can of soup and the sliced
    onion.
4   Simmer for 1 hour, with the lid on the pan.

Notes from test cooking. Ask the butcher to bone the
breast for you – if you ask during a slack shopping time,
he may even cut it up into the 1-inch squares.

If no such service is available, you will need a sharp
knife if you want to bone the breast for yourself.

We experimented by cutting up an unboned breast of
lamb – it had been bought at a supermarket and was just
roughly chopped between the bones. We sliced it into
strips through the butcher's chopping and then cut each
strip across into squares, avoiding the bones: you may
find it easier to leave it in strips. Once it is cooked, it is
easy to cut out the bones as you eat the meat.

Lamb Ragout

Serves 2–3

Oven temperature: 375–400°F, gas mark 5–6

Cooking time: 1 hour approximately

INGREDIENTS

1 breast of lamb, chopped or boned
garlic (optional)

2 medium carrots ⎫
2 medium onions ⎬ peeled and cut into dice
2 medium potatoes⎭
margarine, dripping or lard
rosemary (optional)
seasoning
stock made with water and stock cube (optional)

METHOD

1   Rub the lamb with a cut clove of garlic if you like a
    slight garlic flavour. Cut the lamb – boned or un-
    boned – into small portions.
2   Add the lamb to the vegetables and put into a roast-
    ing tray with a very little fat. If you like, sprinkle with
    a little rosemary as well as salt and pepper.
3   Roast, uncovered, in the oven at 375–400°F, gas
    mark 5–6, stirring every 15 minutes.
4   When the meat and vegetables are beginning to
    brown, cover the tin and continue cooking till tender.
    You may like this rather crisp and dry (watch to
    prevent burning) or you may prefer to add a little
    stock to the tin to make it juicy.

Stuffed Lamb's Heart

This is an economical roast meal for 2

Oven temperature: 325°F, gas mark 3

Cooking time: 2 hours

INGREDIENTS

3 tablespoons dry sage and
onion stuffing mix

6 tablespoons boiling water (or
as stated on the stuffing mix
packet)

1 lamb's heart, left whole

2 oz. dripping

Serve with greens or other favourite vegetable.

METHOD

1 Make the stuffing following the directions on the
packet.

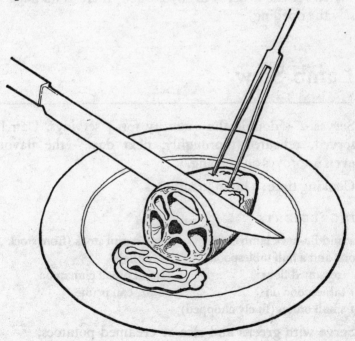

2 Using the tip of your finger, press the stuffing into the
   heart making sure the stuffing is pushed into the tip
   of the heart. There is no need to trim the heart.

3 When the heart is plump and well stuffed, place in a
   small uncovered baking dish with the dripping and
   roast at 325°F, gas mark 3, for 2 hours. Baste the
   heart every half an hour to stop it from drying.

4 A gravy can be made from the meat juices and vegetable water as you would for a roast.

5 Carve thinly from the open end to the tip.

   Note. If the heart is firmly stuffed, there is no need to
sew the opening.

Lamb Stew

Serves 2 – double the quantity for 4 servings. Can be
served, reheated thoroughly, next day – the flavour
even improves on keeping.

Cooking time: 1 hour 30 minutes

INGREDIENTS

4 middle-neck lamb chops
one and a half tablespoons
   seasoned flour
1 tablespoon oil
1 small onion (finely chopped)

half a pint stock (from stock
   cube)
small pinch cinnamon
8-oz. can prunes

Serve with greens and rice or creamed potatoes.

METHOD

1 Coat chops in flour and fry in hot oil until brown both sides.
2 Transfer to large saucepan, add onion, stock and cinnamon and bring to boil.
3 Cover and simmer for 1 hour 30 minutes adding prunes and juice 15 minutes before cooking is completed.

Love Apple Lamb

(Tomatoes were once known as 'love apples'.)

Serves 2

Oven temperature: 350°F, gas mark 4

Cooking time: 1 hour

INGREDIENTS

2 lamb chops
1–2 oz. butter or margarine
seasoning

2 oz. mushrooms
1 onion
2 medium tomatoes

METHOD

1 Wash and trim chops. Brown in butter or margarine, place in casserole and season lightly.
2 Wash and slice mushrooms and sprinkle over chops.

3   Slice onion thinly and place raw over the mushrooms.
4   Place sliced tomatoes on top, season again lightly.
There is no need to add any stock because the juice runs out to give sufficient liquid.
5   Cover with lid or foil and cook at 350°F, gas mark 4, for approximately 1 hour.

Comments from the College of Further Education, Stafford:

Thirteen elderly students tried this recipe.

Thirteen worked from the recipe sheet unaided and liked the recipe very much.

All said they would cook it again at home.

Pronounced a winner!

Leek Soup

Serves 2–3 (2 if this is to be the full meal with bread or toast; 3 if it is a first course)

INGREDIENTS

2 leeks (under half a lb.)   1 oz. grated cheese
one and a half oz. margarine   salt (optional)
a packet of white-sauce mix*   toast
three quarters of a pint milk

    * Buy the size which is usually made up for a sauce with half a pint of milk; our recipe uses three quarters of a pint because

the soup stock needs to be thinner than a sauce – it is thickened by the leeks.

METHOD

1 Trim off the roots and the tough parts of the green of the leeks. Slice the leeks right down in two halves so that they can be well washed free of soil.

2 Cut the washed leeks across into *very* thin slices and cook gently in margarine until tender, about 10 minutes.

3 Off the heat, shower in the sauce mix and gradually stir in the milk.

4 Cook for 3 minutes, stirring constantly.

5 Add the grated cheese and stir, but do not overcook because cheese will become stringy. Taste to decide whether additional salt is needed.

6 Cut the toast into small squares and serve with the soup.

Note from test cooking. If you find it troublesome to grate cheese, replace the white-sauce mix and grated cheese in this recipe with a packet of cheese-sauce mix.

Liver – Quick and Easy

Nutrition note. Liver is a rich source of protein, iron, B vitamins and vitamins A and D. The vitamin C from the lemon juice in this recipe may help the body to absorb iron, so this is a recommended dish for those who tend to be anaemic; also for the housebound and others who cannot get sufficient vitamin D from sunlight.

Serves 2

Cooking time: about 5 minutes

INGREDIENTS

2 or 3 thin slices lamb's or pig's liver
knob of margarine
2 teaspoons cornflour blended with a quarter of a pint (1 teacup) cold milk

salt and pepper
parsley
lemon

METHOD

1   Cut the liver into strips. Using a small saucepan or frying pan, melt the margarine over gentle heat. Add the liver and fry gently in the margarine until lightly cooked (approximately 3 minutes).
2   Spoon the cornflour into a teacup, pour on a little milk and stir till smooth. Stir in the rest of the milk.
3   Pour the cornflour and milk over the liver. Season with salt and pepper.
4   Bring to the boil, stirring all the time. The sauce will thicken slightly.
5   Serve decorated with parsley (chopped or in sprigs) and with wedges of lemon which you squeeze into the sauce on the plate just before eating.

Liver Bake

Serves 2

Oven temperature: 350°F, gas mark 4

Cooking time: 45 minutes

INGREDIENTS

4 oz. liver
salt and pepper

4 oz. tomatoes, sliced
1–2 rashers bacon

Stuffing

1 oz. fresh white breadcrumbs
half an oz. shredded suet
1 heaped teaspoon chopped
parsley
grated rind of quarter to half
a lemon

small egg, beaten
quarter of a teaspoon dried
mixed herbs

Suggestion: Serve with a green vegetable.

METHOD

1 Wash the liver well and cut into quarter-inch slices.
2 Mix all the stuffing ingredients together.
3 In a small greased ovenproof dish, place alternate layers of liver, seasoning, stuffing and tomatoes. Lay the bacon rashers on top.
4 Cover with kitchen foil or a lid.
5 Bake for 45 minutes at 350°F, gas mark 4, removing the foil or lid towards the end of the baking time.

Macaroni Cheese Special

Serves 2

INGREDIENTS

2 oz. quick-cooking macaroni
1–2 rashers streaky bacon,
   fried to crisp
3 small tomatoes, skinned,
   sliced and lightly fried

Just under half a pint cheese
   sauce (see page 129)
a little extra grated cheese

METHOD

1 Bring 1 pint of salted water to a fast boil. Sprinkle in the quick-cooking macaroni, bring back to the boil. Stir.

2 While waiting for the macaroni to cook, fry the bacon and tomatoes.

3 After 7 minutes, test the macaroni for 'doneness' (just soft enough to bite, not mushy). Remove from heat and drain.

4 Take a heatproof casserole dish, put in a layer of macaroni, cover with half the cheese sauce.

5 Sprinkle on half the cut-up bacon, and half the tomato.

6 Add the rest of the macaroni and cheese sauce.

7 Decorate with the rest of the bacon and tomato.

8 Sprinkle on a little grated cheese and place under a medium grill to heat and brown.

Meat Balls

Serves 2

INGREDIENTS

half a lb. raw minced beef
salt, pepper, nutmeg
flour
oil or dripping for frying

1 small can tomatoes
1 teaspoon gravy powder and
  1 teacup cold water, mixed
  together

METHOD

1   Mix the raw mince and seasoning in a little flour.
2   Roll into meat balls.
3   Melt the oil or dripping in a saucepan and, when hot, add the meat balls. Cook, turning frequently, till browned all over.
4   Add the tomatoes, roughly chopped, with their juice and the gravy liquid.
5   Bring to the boil, stir, then cover with a lid and simmer for 30–40 minutes.

Serve with (a) boiled spaghetti or noodles OR (b) boiled rice OR (c) potatoes.

Meat Loaf

Serves 2, or can make 1 hot serving, 1 cold serving next day

Oven temperature: 350°F, gas mark 4

Cooking time: approximately 1 hour

INGREDIENTS

quarter of a lb. minced beef
quarter of a lb. sausage meat
1 dessertspoon chopped onion
1 dessertspoon chopped
  parsley

pinch mixed herbs
2 tablespoons fresh
  breadcrumbs or crumbled
  stale bread
1 egg

METHOD

1 Mix all ingredients together, binding with the beaten egg.
2 *Either* press into a small greased loaf tin *or* grease a strip of greaseproof paper and wrap it around the roll to hold it in shape, then wrap in kitchen foil and put on to a baking tray.
3 Bake for 1 hour at 350°F, gas mark 4, just above the centre of the oven.
4 Cut into two to four pieces and lift carefully on to a dish.

Note. This can be served with roast potatoes or favourite vegetables and gravy. It gives you a roast meat dinner without any wastage through bones and fat.

One-stage Sauce

You will find this simple method of cooking a sauce produces a quick, smooth sauce, without the bother of first making a roux (see Glossary, page 238).

Use a wooden spoon or a wire whisk (the loop type is illustrated on page 169 of *Easy Cooking for One or Two*).

INGREDIENTS

half a pint milk   1 oz. margarine or butter
1 oz. plain flour   pinch of salt, pepper, mustard

METHOD

1   Put all the ingredients into a small pan. It is not even necessary to sieve the flour, unless you feel happier doing so. Stir well.
2   Let it stand without cooking for a minute in order to allow the flour to soften in the milk.
3   Heat fairly gently, stirring or whisking continuously, and cook until boiling and thick.

For Cheese Sauce

4   Stir in 2–3 oz. strong Cheddar cheese, grated. Do not reboil, or the cheese will be overcooked. There should be enough heat in the sauce to melt the cheese.

Other Variations to Plain One-stage Sauce:

Add chopped parsley *or*
sliced, fried button mushrooms *or*
chopped hard-boiled egg and chives *or*
anchovy essence and a squeeze of lemon juice *or*
capers and a little lemon juice.

Fried or Grilled Plaice

Serves 1

INGREDIENTS

1 *small* plaice (about half a   salt and pepper
    lb.)   butter or margarine
flour   lemon

METHOD

For fried plaice

1   Wash the fish and pat dry.
2   Put a tablespoon or so of flour into a clean paper bag
    and shake in some pepper and salt. Put the plaice into
    the bag and shake gently so that it becomes coated
    with the seasoned flour. (Or put the seasoned flour
    on to a large plate and turn the fish in it to coat it –
    the paper-bag method is less messy on the hands.)

3 Fry gently in butter or margarine for about 10 minutes turning once with a fish slice or palette knife.
4 Serve with a wedge of fresh lemon.

Note. Small plaice are often cheaper per pound than the larger sizes, so if you are serving 2 people it might be more economical to buy 2 small plaice rather than 1 larger fish. These small plaice are best left on the bone – the flesh comes off the bones easily once it is cooked. There is no need to bother with egg and breadcrumbs for coating unless you want to – they are attractive merely dipped in seasoned flour and fried in butter or margarine as directed above.

For grilled plaice

After washing and patting the fish dry, grease the grill pan well. Then merely season the fish, dot with butter or margarine and grill gently under moderate heat for about 10–15 minutes, turning once with a fish slice or palette knife.

For steamed fish

See Glossary, page 242.

Baked Pork Chop

Serves 1

Oven temperature: 250°–275°F, gas mark 1

Cooking time: approximately 1 hour 30 minutes

INGREDIENTS

1 pork chop	1 tomato
half an oz. lard	1 small onion
salt and pepper	1 apple
flour	

METHOD

1 Remove rind from chop. Put rind and lard into pan and heat gently until fat runs from the rind.

2 Season and flour chop.

3 Fry in fat 3–4 minutes each side. Keep this pan for frying vegetables later.

4 Place chop in greased ovenproof dish, cover and bake at 250°–275°F, gas mark 1 for 1 hour 30 minutes.

5 Towards the end of cooking, peel and chop the tomato, onion and apple. Season and cook gently, uncovered, in the pan the chop was cooked in.

6 Serve the chop on top of the vegetables.

Recipe sent from 'Cooking for One or Two' class, College of Adult Education, Wolverhampton. Comment: 'Most tender chop ever eaten! Slow cooking made it moist – many pork chops tend to be dry when eaten.'

Curried Pork

Serves 2 – double the quantities for 4 servings

INGREDIENTS

half a lb. lean left-over cooked
   pork, diced,
or
half a lb. uncooked pork pieces
1 small onion (finely chopped)
2 tablespoons oil
1 level tablespoon curry
   powder

good pinch ground ginger
just over a quarter of a pint
   stock (from stock cube)
1 small cooking apple (peeled
   and diced)
1 dessertspoon sultanas
quarter of a teaspoon salt
3 oz. long-grain rice (washed)

Serve with chutney, plain yogurt and diced fresh
cucumber.

METHOD

1 Gently fry onion in oil until soft and turning golden.
2 Add curry powder and ginger and stir rapidly to fry
   for a couple of minutes.
3 At this stage, if using uncooked pork, add to the onion
   mixture and fry, stirring, for a few minutes. The
   cooked pork does not need this preliminary frying.
4 Add meat, stock, apple, sultanas and salt. Bring to the
   boil. Reduce heat, cover and simmer for 15 minutes (if
   using uncooked pork, simmer for 40 minutes).
5 Add rice and simmer gently until all the liquid is
   absorbed (about 20 minutes)

6 Curried pork is best served with a mango chutney, plain yogurt and – for colour and freshness – diced unpeeled cucumber.

Comment from 'Over 60s' class: 'Mmmm – rather hot but goes down a treat. Very digestible.'

Belly of Pork, Grilled

Serves 2–3

INGREDIENTS

approximately 1 lb. lean belly of pork, in rashers (see step 1 below)

garlic powder
soy sauce

Can be served with: potatoes and red cabbage (see page 188).

METHOD

1 Have the belly of pork cut into rashers by the butcher.
2 Sprinkle well with garlic powder and soy sauce.
3 Grill till very crisp – this may take 30–40 minutes.

Pamela's Potato Soup

Serves 2

INGREDIENTS

1 large potato
1 small onion
a little margarine

half a herb-flavoured stock
   cube (see step 3 below).
three quarters of a pint water

METHOD

1   Peel the potato and onion and cut into small dice.

2   In a small saucepan, fry the vegetables gently in the margarine for a few minutes so that they absorb the fat and develop a tasty flavour.

3   Add the water and half a herb-flavoured stock cube (or chicken stock cube plus a pinch of mixed herbs). Bring to the boil, stirring occasionally.

4   Put the lid on the pan and simmer very gently for approximately 10 minutes – just till the vegetables are soft.

Rabbit in Beer

Serves 2

INGREDIENTS

2 portions of rabbit
seasoning
1 small onion, chopped
butter and oil for frying

1 small orange, sliced unpeeled
quarter of a pint beer
    (preferably brown ale)
pinch of mixed herbs

METHOD

1   In a small saucepan, fry the seasoned rabbit and onion
    until the rabbit is browned all over.
2   Add the orange, beer and mixed herbs and simmer
    for 1 hour 30 minutes.

Note from test cooking. If you like a slightly thickened
gravy, dip the rabbit joints in seasoned flour before
frying.

Rhubarb and Orange Crumble or Rhubarb and Apple Crumble

Serves 2 – or makes one hot serving and one cold serving for the next day

Oven temperature: 350°F, gas mark 4

Cooking time: 35 minutes

INGREDIENTS

3 oz. flour
one and a half oz. soft
  margarine
one and a half oz. demerara or
  granulated sugar
8 oz. rhubarb

1 small orange
or
1 small eating apple
1–2 tablespoons granulated
  sugar
water

METHOD

1 Put the flour and soft margarine into a mixing bowl and gently mash and stir, or rub with the fingertips, till it is the consistency of large breadcrumbs. Stir in the one and a half oz. sugar.
2 Wash the rhubarb and cut small (about 1-inch lengths). Put in an ovenproof dish.
3 *Either* peel the orange and cut the flesh into small pieces *or* peel and core the apple and cut up small.
4 Mix the 1–2 tablespoons of sugar and the orange or apple into the rhubarb. With the orange add 1

teaspoon water. With the apple add 1 tablespoon water.
5   Sprinkle the crumble thickly over the top.
6   Bake at 350°F, gas mark 4, for approximately 35 minutes.

Note from test cooking. An easy crumble can be made by using soft margarine and mashing it into the flour with a fork. If you use a hard margarine you will need to rub fat in to flour. Stir in the sugar.

Store-cupboard alternative. Use canned rhubarb, canned mandarin oranges and *very little* of their juice. If you like, you can use a crumble mix for the topping.

Risotto

Serves 2

INGREDIENTS

1 small onion, chopped
1 stick celery, chopped*
knob of dripping
3–4 oz. raw minced meat
2–3 oz. long-grain rice
   (uncooked)

1 small can of tomatoes
quarter of a pint water
salt and pepper
good pinch of herbs

METHOD

1 Fry the onion and celery in the dripping for a few
   minutes, until soft.
2 Add the meat and fry, stirring until lightly browned.
3 Stir in the rice and continue frying for a further few
   minutes.
4 Pour in the tomatoes with their juice and the water,
   breaking up the tomatoes roughly with a spoon or
   fork. Add the seasonings and herbs.
5 Bring to the boil, cover and simmer gently until the
   meat is tender, the rice soft and the liquid absorbed
   (approximately 15–20 minutes). Taste for seasoning.

* To use the rest of the head of celery: Serve it *braised* (see the
companion volume of this book, *Easy Cooking for One or Two*,
page 55), or *boiled* as a vegetable, or in Ham and Celery Mornay,
page 57, or *chopped up raw* in a celery and cheese salad or a
sandwich.

Saucer Wholemeal Tart

Serves 1 (can be served hot or cold)
Oven temperature: 375°F, gas mark 5
Cooking time: approximately 25 minutes

INGREDIENTS

1 oz. wholemeal flour
pinch of salt

2 teaspoons cooking oil
2 teaspoons water

Filling .

1 egg
salt and pepper
pinch of oregano (optional)
2 teaspoons milk
2 teaspoons finely chopped
  leek or onion
1 oz. Cheddar or similar
  cheese, finely sliced

chopped parsley
1 small tomato (sliced)
(other ingredients, e.g.
  cooked vegetables, bacon or
  ham can be added to vary
  this recipe)

You will need an old china saucer to use instead of a baking tin.

METHOD

1 With a knife or pastry blender mix together the flour, salt, oil and water to form a soft dough.
2 There is no need to roll this dough, merely press it with the fingers into the saucer so that it is thinly lined with the pastry.
3 Beat together the egg, seasonings and milk.
4 Sprinkle the finely chopped raw leek or onion over

the pastry. Top with the slices of cheese and plenty of parsley.

5   Pour the egg and milk mixture into the saucer.
6   Decorate with slices of tomato.
7   For ease of handling, put the saucer onto a baking tray before putting it into the oven at 375°F, gas mark 5. The pastry and filling should be cooked and turning slightly golden in about 25 minutes.

Note. This is an easy-going recipe; you can vary the ingredients for the filling according to your larder.

Scone Pizza

Serves 2 (halve quantities for 1)

Oven temperature: 425°F, gas mark 7

Cooking time: 25–30 minutes (same time for half quantity)

INGREDIENTS

Scone

6 oz. shortcrust pastry mix
   (or 2 oz. margarine or
   butter rubbed into 4 oz.
   plain flour)
1 rounded teaspoon baking
   powder

pinch of mustard
pinch of mixed herbs
milk or water to mix

Topping

1 kipper fillet *or* 1 slice streaky   salt and pepper
   bacon   2 oz. Cheddar cheese, grated
3 canned tomatoes   or thinly sliced

METHOD

1   Stir pastry mix (or rubbed-in fat and flour) together
    with baking powder, mustard and herbs. Add milk or

water to make a scone consistency (i.e. a soft but
not sticky dough).

2   Pat into round scone shape, less than half an inch
thick. Place on greased baking tray.

3   If using kipper, pour boiling water over the kipper
fillet in a deep dish and leave for 2 minutes before
removing from the water. Skin and slit into long
strips. OR cut raw bacon into strips.

4   Drain the tomatoes from juice, slice them and place
two thirds onto scone. Season.

5   Arrange cheese over top. Place strips of kipper or
bacon to decorate on top of pizza. Place pieces of
tomato between strips.

6   Bake at 425°F, gas mark 7, until firm and golden.
Serve hot.

Shortcrust Pastry

There are several different methods for making shortcrust pastry. Some of them are mentioned on pages 144–7
of *Easy Cooking for One or Two*. Two more of my favourite
methods, using margarine, are given on pages 182–5 of
Easy Cooking for Three or More.

The recipe below is a traditional one, using half
margarine and half lard.

INGREDIENTS
(*Note.* This is made in the proportion of half fats to flour.

If a larger amount is required, use 2 oz. margarine, 2 oz.
lard to 8 oz. flour, and extra water.)

6 oz. plain flour   one and a half oz. lard
a pinch of salt   cold water to mix
one and a half oz. margarine   (approximately 6 teaspoons)

METHOD

1   Sieve the flour and salt into a mixing bowl.
2   Add the fats and cut into small pieces with a round
    bladed knife – see illustration, page 240.
3   Rub the fats gently but firmly into the flour with the
    finger tips and thumb tips of both hands, lifting the
    hands up from the bowl so that air gets into the mix-
    ture – see illustration, page 241.
4   When the mixture resembles large breadcrumbs, take
    the bowl by the rim with both hands, and swish it
    round on the table so that the larger lumps swish up
    to the top. Rub them in a little more.
5   Sprinkle the water over the mixture and stir it in
    with the knife until the mixture begins to stick to-
    gether.
6   Gather together with the hand and knead it lightly for
    a few seconds till smooth – it can be turned out onto a
    floured board or table and pressed into shape with
    the knuckles before rolling it out with light strokes
    (do not pull or stretch).

Note. Usual thickness: about one eighth of an inch.
Usual oven temperature: 425°F, gas mark 7.

Suet Crust Pastry

INGREDIENTS

(*Note*. This is generally made in the proportion of half suet to flour, i.e. 3 oz. suet to 6 oz. flour, or 4 oz. suet to 8 oz. flour.)

6 oz. self-raising flour

or

6 oz. plain flour plus 3 level teaspoons baking powder

pinch of salt
3 oz. shredded suet
cold water to mix

METHOD

1 Sieve the flour (or flour and baking powder) with the salt into the mixing bowl.
2 Stir in the suet.
3 Gradually pour in a little water, stirring it rapidly round with the blade of a knife so that it begins to mix together. (The amount of water required varies according to the flour used.)
4 Gather together with your hand to make a firm dough.
5 Knead lightly, then roll out to the shape required.

Spanish Omelette

Serves 2

Note. You could also add a tablespoon of cooked peas, carrots or mushrooms, or chopped cooked ham. This would not then be a traditional Spanish Omelette but it does make a more substantial meal. Some Spanish omelettes include lightly fried onions.

INGREDIENTS

half an oz. butter or margarine   half a level teaspoon salt
2 small boiled potatoes, diced   shake of pepper
4 standard eggs

METHOD

1 Heat butter or margarine in frying pan (about 7 inches in diameter).
2 Add diced potatoes and cook till golden brown.
3 Beat eggs lightly and add seasoning.
4 Add eggs to potato and hot fat, and stir lightly to distribute the potato fairly evenly. Then cook as for an ordinary omelette (i.e. when the egg is just beginning to set at the bottom, use a fork or palette knife and draw the mixture to the middle from the sides, so that the runny egg will cook. Repeat, but it is ready to serve when the top is still slightly runny.)
5 *Either* fold in two and serve

or

(the Spanish way) place the pan under a hot grill for
a few moments only, just enough to set the top without hardening it. Slip the omelette, flat, onto a plate
and divide it into two servings.

Spiced Apple Purée

Serves 2

INGREDIENTS

1 lb. cooking apples
quarter to a half teaspoon
   ground cinnamon
quarter to a half teaspoon
   ground mixed spice

a generous pinch ground
   ginger
a little honey
mandarin yogurt (optional)

METHOD

1 Peel, quarter and core the apples and cook very
   gently with the minimum of water. Keep the lid on
   the saucepan but peep occasionally to make sure the
   apples are not burning.
2 Add the spices and honey, a little at a time, tasting to
   get the mixture of spice and sweet which most appeals
   to you. Serve hot or cold.
3 This is particularly nice topped with a spoonful of

mandarin yogurt, or you may prefer the top of the milk.

Note from test cooking. I generally reckon 1 tablespoon of water for every apple but this varies according to the variety of apple – if it is not enough add a little more water. Keeping the apples in quarters and not sweetening until later makes them go into a fluffy purée fairly quickly – probably in about 10 minutes – but this again varies with apple variety and size. Pound them with a spoon if necessary to help them to break down to a smooth purée.

Tomato and Basil Salad

INGREDIENTS

firm tomatoes*   French dressing (page 206)
dried or fresh basil

   * Misshapen 'salad' tomatoes can often be bought cheaper than the rest, and, once they are sliced up, who notices their shape?

METHOD

1   Scald (see Glossary) the tomatoes if you want to peel them, but they can merely be washed and left unpeeled. Slice them with a sharp knife.

2 Put them in layers in the salad bowl, sprinkling each
   layer generously with chopped basil and French dressing.
3 Leave for a short while for the flavours to mingle.

Vegetable Stew

Serves 2 or more

INGREDIENTS

a handful of dried pulse   a knob of butter or margarine
  vegetables (e.g. peas,   salt and pepper
  lentils, red beans)   dried oregano (optional)
a mixture of vegetables in   mixed herbs
  season   tomato purée

METHOD

1 Cook the pulse vegetables in water in a small pan till
   almost tender (some cook quicker if they are first
   soaked overnight – cooking time depends on the
   variety you choose, and instructions are usually on
   the packet).
2 Cut up a mixture of fresh vegetables – the more
   variety the better. In a large saucepan, fry the vegetables for 2 or 3 minutes in a little butter or margarine.
3 Add the cooked dried vegetables and liquid (or a
   little stock) and continue simmering till all are
   cooked.

4   Flavour with seasonings and herbs, and buck up the flavour and colour by stirring in a little tomato purée.

Note. Left-over raw vegetables can be used to make Woolton Pie (page 197) next day.

Chapter 4
Cooking for Companionship

Some people, without company, fall into the trap of not bothering to cook for one. A shared meal can buck up their appetite. It is my conviction that even bread and cheese tastes better if eaten in the company of a friend. Thinking like this, it was difficult for me to select recipes for a chapter called 'Cooking for Companionship'. Any of the recipes in this book – even the simplest in the 'Non-cooks' chapter – could be enjoyed in company. So I decided to pick out, in addition to the others:

1. Some recipes which may be wasteful to cook for only one.

2. My 'party pieces' – very deceptive all of them because, although they may look elaborate, they are *very* easy to cook.

Apple and Ginger Upside-down Cake

Serves 4 as a warm pudding. Or it can be left to get cold and will then serve 5–6 smaller slices as a cake. For 2 people, serve half of it, warm, one day and the other half, cold, the next day.

Oven temperature: 325°F, gas mark 3

Cooking time: 25–35 minutes

INGREDIENTS

Topping

1 medium cooking apple
1 glacé cherry
2 oz. (4 level tablespoons) brown sugar

1 oz. margarine
1 level teaspoon ground ginger

Cake

2 oz. soft margarine
2 oz. caster sugar
1 egg, large and unbeaten

2 oz. self-raising flour
half a level teaspoon baking powder

You will need a round sponge sandwich tin.

METHOD

1 Well grease the sponge sandwich tin.
2 Peel, quarter, core and slice the apple in *very* thin slices and place in tin, overlapping the slices around the tin. Place two cherry halves in the centre.

3   Melt the brown sugar, margarine and ginger in a
     small saucepan and spoon over the top of the apple
     slices. (When the cake is turned out of the tin, this will
     form the 'topping'.)
4   Place all the cake ingredients together in a bowl (if
     you have a sieve, the flour and baking powder can be
     sieved in together, but I have made a perfectly
     satisfactory cake without sieving). Beat with a wooden
     spoon until well mixed. This is very easy to do and will
     only take a couple of minutes.
5   Spread carefully over the apple and sugar.
6   Bake in a preheated oven 325°F, gas mark 3, on the
     middle shelf for 25–35 minutes.
7   Turn out carefully onto the serving plate.

Apple Pastry Cake

Serves 6

Oven temperature: 425°F, gas mark 7

Cooking time: approximately 35 minutes

INGREDIENTS

seven-and-a-half-oz. packet
  frozen puff pastry, thawed
half a lb. cooking apples
one and a half oz. granulated
  sugar

2 heaped tablespoons apricot
  jam
whipping or double cream
  (optional)

You will need a shallow baking sheet or tin.

METHOD

1 Roll out pastry to a thin oblong, smaller than the baking sheet, and trim the edges straight with a knife. Dampen the baking sheet with a little water and lift the pastry onto it (this helps to prevent the pastry sticking).

2 Peel and slice the apples fairly thinly, and arrange the slices on the pastry.

3 Bake in the centre of the preheated oven for 25 minutes.

4 Take the pastry cake out of the oven and sprinkle the sugar over the apples.

5 Put back in the oven for another 10 minutes, or until cooked through.

6 As soon as it comes out of the oven, spread jam over the top of the apples. Eat the day that it is made. It is nicest eaten warm (optional: with whipped cream on top).

Batch Baking Day

Prepare the scones, buns and pastry squares in one session, and bake all in the oven together on lightly-greased baking tins.

Oven temperature: 425°F, gas mark 7

Cooking time: approximately 15 minutes

INGREDIENTS

Basic mixture

12 oz. self-raising flour
four and a half oz. soft
  margarine

four and a half oz. sugar
2 small eggs or 1 large egg
a little milk

For scones (makes 5)

1 tablespoon extra flour
a little more milk, if necessary

a few currants and raisins *or*
  a little mixed dried fruit

For rock buns (makes 6)

a little desiccated coconut

For jam buns (makes 5)

a little jam

For pastry squares (makes 9)

a little jam

a little icing sugar

METHOD

1 Rub margarine into flour, stir in sugar and mix to a
   stiff pastry with the eggs beaten into a little milk.
2 Divide into four. Use the first quarter for:

Scones

3 Knead in 1 tablespoon more flour and enough milk to
   make a soft scone consistency. It can be left plain,
   but for fruit scones gently knead in a little dried fruit.
4 *Either*, pat into a round, about half an inch thick; with

the blunt side of a knife mark deeply into wedge
shapes.

Or, roll out half an inch thick and cut into rounds
with a 2-inch cutter.

5   Brush the top with milk if you wish (this gives the
cooked scones a nice browned finish).

Rock Buns

6   Take the next quarter of the mixture. Add a little
desiccated coconut and knead lightly. With your
hands, roll it into six little rock buns.

Jam Buns

7   Use the next quarter for jam buns: roll into pastry
balls, press a hole in the middles with your finger and
fill with jam. Either press over the top to enclose the
jam completely, or leave a little jam showing through
the top.

Pastry Squares

8   Take the last quarter of the mixture and roll it out,
keeping it as square as possible. Trim the edges neatly.

9   Spread the pastry with jam. Bake this square with the
buns and scones at 425°F, gas mark 7 for approximately 15 minutes.

10 When the pastry square is cooked and nearly cool,
sprinkle with icing sugar and cut into nine dainty
little squares.

11 Cool scones, buns and squares on wire racks.

Beef Stroganoff

Serves 3–4. Halve quantities for 2 servings.

INGREDIENTS

1 lb. good quality minced beef
salt, pepper
4 oz. butter (*or* 2 oz. butter
   and 2 fluid oz. oil)
1 onion, skinned and diced
4 oz. mushrooms, sliced
half an oz. flour
   (1 dessertspoon)
1 tablespoon tomato purée

half a teaspoon made mustard
1 teaspoon paprika
half a pint sour cream or plain
   yogurt
1 tablespoon brandy or
   quarter of a pint red wine
   (optional)
parsley (optional)

METHOD

1   Season the minced beef with salt and pepper.
2   Heat the butter (or butter and oil) in a pan, add the onion and cook till it becomes transparent.
3   Add the mushrooms and stir around to cook lightly.
4   Remove the onions and mushrooms from the pan, reheat the fat, then add the meat and cook quickly till just browned.
5   Return the onions and mushrooms to the meat, add the flour, then blend in the tomato purée, mustard, paprika and sour cream. (If the red wine is used pour in as well.)
6   Simmer *gently* till the meat is tender, stirring from time to time to prevent burning (approximately 45 minutes).

7   If brandy is used, add it towards the end of the cook-
    ing period.
8   Serve in a hot dish sprinkled with parsley.

Accompaniments :

(a) New potatoes or rice or spaghetti.
(b) Green salad or broccoli spears or French beans.

Note from test cooking. At today's prices, this is not a
cheap dish but it is more economical than using the
traditional best quality fillet of beef. It is a rich dish, so
serve something light and tart after it, e.g. Orange Juice
Jelly (p. 214), Spiced Apple Purée (p. 147).

Beetroot and Mint Salad

INGREDIENTS

cooked beetroot (fresh, not   plain yogurt
    pickled)   dried or fresh mint

METHOD

1   Slice or dice the peeled cooked beetroot.
2   Stir with a few tablespoons of plain yogurt (which will
    go an attractive bright pink).
3   Just before serving, sprinkle with dried mint, or
    sprinkle with chopped fresh mint (the leaves are
    easily 'chopped' by snipping with scissors).

Chicken and Orange Casserole

This recipe is one of several contributed to this book from The Elms Technical College, Stoke-on-Trent. My thanks to the teachers and students of the course on 'Practical Nutrition for Retired People'.

Serves 1 or 2

Oven temperature: 350°F, gas mark 4

Cooking time: 1 hour, after preliminary cooking, which may take 15–20 minutes

INGREDIENTS

1–2 chicken joints
seasoned flour (see Glossary)
1 oz. butter
1 oz. mushrooms, sliced
2 oz. onions, sliced
1 oz. flour
half a pint stock or water

juice and grated rind of half
   an orange
extra seasoning (optional)
small bay leaf
a tablespoon frozen or tinned
   peas for garnish (optional)

Can be served with extra vegetables or salad.

METHOD

1 Coat the chicken joints with seasoned flour. Fry chicken in butter for about 10 minutes and transfer to casserole.
2 Fry the mushrooms and onions lightly in pan and add to casserole.

3   Add the 1 oz. flour to the fat in the pan and heat
    gently, stirring, to brown slightly. Gradually stir in
    the stock, and the juice and rind of orange and bring
    to the boil. Taste for seasoning.
4   Pour over the chicken in the casserole. Add bay leaf.
    Cover and cook at 350°F, gas mark 4, for 1 hour (or
    simmer in saucepan or flameproof casserole on top of
    the stove instead of in the oven). Garnish with cooked
    peas and serve.

Chicken Special

Suitable for breast of chicken or boned-out chicken thigh.

Serves 2

Oven temperature: 375–400°F, gas mark 5–6

Cooking time: approximately 35 minutes

INGREDIENTS

2 small boned chicken joints
pinch mixed herbs in a few
    white breadcrumbs with
    salt and pepper
or
1 dessertspoon packet stuffing
    (used dry)

lemon juice
2 rashers smoked streaky bacon

METHOD

1 Flatten the chicken joints slightly, place stuffing or herbs and breadcrumbs in boned cavity or under breast fillet.
2 Sprinkle with plenty of lemon juice.
3 Remove bacon rind and press rashers with the flat of a knife blade to make them thinner and longer. Wrap bacon neatly around chicken joints.
4 Sprinkle with a little extra white crumb or stuffing.
5 Bake in oven at 375–400°F, gas mark 5–6, for about 35 minutes.
6 Serve hot with gravy made with the chicken and bacon juices.

Notes from 'Over 60s' cookery class. This dish is also very good cold. It is popular with our members. The light herb flavouring can be varied with the different dried and garden herbs available, or of course various spices make a change.

Dips and Dunks

A dip is a soft, well-flavoured mixture. A dunk is a bite-size portion of something firm or crisp which can be 'dunked' and eaten – using fingers, not cutlery.

INGREDIENTS

Quick and easy dips

1 large carton plain yogurt

half a packet dried soup-powder; you can make several different
dips by varying the soup used, e.g. asparagus, mushroom,
tomato or onion flavour.

Dunks

raw vegetables (e.g. carrots, cauliflower, celery)
crisps or small savoury biscuits

Note. For a small amount, use a small carton of plain yogurt, and less soup mix.

METHOD

1 Empty the yogurt into a bowl.
2 Shake in the dry soup powder, a little at a time, stirring it with a fork until it is well mixed and the flavour to your liking.
3 Wash and prepare the vegetables, i.e. cut carrots and celery into strips or slices, divide the white of cauliflower into its small flowerets.

Easter Ring

Oven temperature: 400–425°F, gas mark 6–7

Cooking time: approximately 25 minutes

INGREDIENTS

1 small packet puff pastry
   (thawed)
half a pound packet marzipan
   (or almond paste)

2 oz. icing sugar
12 almonds or walnuts
6 glacé cherries

METHOD

1 Roll the pastry thinly into a long strip and damp the edges with water.

2   Roll the marzipan into a 'sausage', the same length
    as the pastry strip.
3   Place the marzipan on the pastry and roll up, damp-
    ing edges to seal.
4   Form this roll into a circle. Place, with the join under-
    neath, on a wetted baking sheet (to prevent sticking)
    and slit the top of the pastry with short sloping cuts.

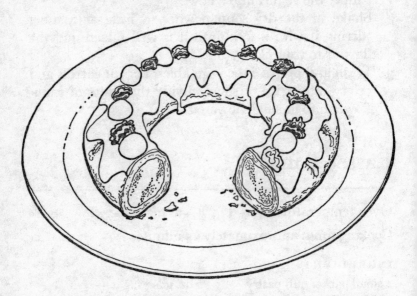

5   Bake at 400–425°F, gas mark 6–7, until golden brown
    and cooked right through, approximately 25 minutes.
6   When cool mix the icing sugar with a few drops of
    water to make a glacé icing and pour and spread over
    the top of the ring.
7   Decorate the top with nuts and cherries.

Easy-mix Christmas Cake

Recipe sent to me from the College of Further Education, Stafford, by Mrs Jean Smallwood, who runs a class for retired students.

Oven temperature: 275–300°F, gas mark 1–2

Cooking time: 2 hours 30 minutes

INGREDIENTS

4 oz. plain flour
half a level teaspoon baking
    powder
quarter of a teaspoon nutmeg
quarter of a teaspoon mixed
    spice
quarter of a teaspoon
    cinnamon
4 oz. soft creaming margarine
4 oz. soft brown sugar
2 eggs
5 oz. currants

3 oz. raisins
3 oz. sultanas
1 oz. mixed peel
1 oz. glacé cherries
1 oz. ground almonds
2 drops almond essence
grated rind of half a lemon
juice of quarter of a lemon
1 teaspoon black treacle
brandy, rum or sherry
    (optional)

You will need a 6 inch cake tin (see Glossary for greasing and lining).

METHOD

1   Sieve flour with baking powder and spices into bowl. Add all the other ingredients except the alcohol (eggs can be left unbeaten) and mix until smooth and well blended.

2   Place in lined 6-inch cake tin. Smooth top level.

3   Bake in centre of oven at 275–300°F, gas mark 1–2, for approximately 2 hours 30 minutes.

4   When cold, turn upside down, make holes with a fine skewer and spoon over 2 tablespoons of chosen alcohol (if desired) : brandy, rum or sherry are suitable.

Can be covered with 8 oz. almond paste, or simply iced with the following:

'Easy-on' Icing

INGREDIENTS

10–12 oz. icing sugar, sieved
1 egg white
1 tablespoon liquid glucose (or

1 dessertspoon golden syrup)
2 tablespoons apricot jam

METHOD

1   Place sugar, egg white and glucose or syrup in mixing bowl and work to a stiff paste with a wooden spoon. Knead well. (Sugar amount will vary slightly according to size of egg white.)

2   Spread cake with jam all over.

3   Roll out icing and lift on to cake.

4   Mould all over the cake (very easily moulded).

5   Polish top with finger dipped in cornflour.

6   Any left-over paste can be coloured and shaped to decorate cake.

Notes from test cooking. This was the easiest-to-mix rich fruit cake I have ever made. The soft creaming margarine is essential – you could not do this 'all-in-one' method with a harder fat.

Because we found it hard to obtain liquid glucose for the icing we substituted golden syrup. This makes it sweeter, so you use less.

I found mixing the icing with a wooden spoon was slightly harder work, but, as soon as most of the icing sugar had been beaten in, I kneaded by hand and then it was very easy – a good recipe. Dust the table or board and the rolling pin with a little sifted icing sugar before you roll out the icing, to prevent it sticking.

Easy-mix Simnel Cake

This was the second easy-mix cake recipe sent by Mrs Jean Smallwood – it proved very popular with the students in her Retirement Class.

Oven temperature: 275–300°F, gas mark 1–2

Cooking time: 2 hours 30 minutes

INGREDIENTS

4 oz. plain flour
3 oz. soft creaming margarine
3 oz. granulated sugar
2 eggs
4 oz. raisins
4 oz. currants
4 oz. sultanas

1 oz. glacé cherries, cut up
8 oz. packet of almond paste
1 tablespoon apricot jam or syrup
beaten egg to glaze
water icing

You will need a 6-inch cake tin (see Glossary for greasing and lining).

METHOD

1   Sieve flour into bowl. Add margarine, sugar, eggs and fruit and mix with a wooden spoon until smooth. (Eggs can be added unbeaten.)
2   Place half the mixture in the lined 6-inch cake tin.

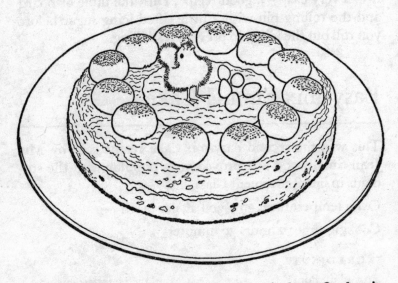

3   Roll half the almond paste to a circle to fit the tin and place on top of cake mixture.
4   Fill the tin with the rest of the cake mixture. Smooth with a knife.
5   Bake in centre of oven for approximately 2 hours 30 minutes at 275–300°F, gas mark 1–2. The cake

feels firm and begins to shrink from the sides of the tin when it is cooked; if you test for 'doneness' with a skewer or knife, remember it may be slightly sticky with the centre layer of almond paste.

6   Turn out cake, remove lining paper, and cool the cake on a wire tray.

7   When cool, brush outer edge of cake with jam or syrup. Divide remaining 4 oz. of almond paste into 12 small balls and place round edge of cake. Flatten slightly with knife.

8   Brush with beaten egg and grill lightly until golden brown.

9   Fill centre of top of cake with small quantity of water icing (2 heaped tablespoons of icing sugar mixed with cold water or lemon juice).

10 Decorate with fluffy toy chickens or other suitable spring-like decorations.

Gooseberry Stuffing

To serve with roast lamb or roast pork.

Serves 2

Oven temperature: 350°F, gas mark 4

Cooking time: 30–40 minutes

INGREDIENTS

approx. 6 oz. canned   half a teaspoon cinnamon
  gooseberries   2 teaspoons brown sugar
6 tablespoons white   salt and pepper
  breadcrumbs   dripping

METHOD

1 Mix all ingredients, except dripping, together.
2 Grease a heatproof dish, fill with the stuffing and dot
   the top with small knobs of dripping.
3 Roast with the joint for the last half hour or so.

Note. This stuffing can also be used to stuff loosely into
a boned joint. You will probably need to halve the
ingredients for a very small joint. Roast at the time and
temperature recommended for the joint.

Grapefruit Appetizer

Serves 1 or 2 or more

The green on top of the yellow looks refreshing and the
sharpness of the dressing makes this a simple appetizer to
serve as a first course for lunch. It is rich in vitamin C.

INGREDIENTS

half a grapefruit per person   fresh mint *or* fresh parsely *or* a
1 teaspoon French dressing   spring onion
  (see recipe, page 206)

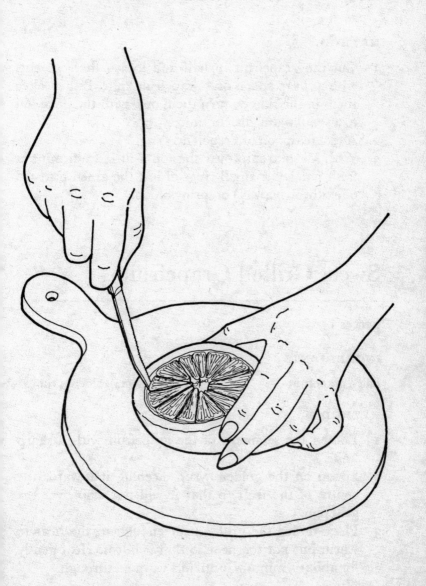

METHOD

1   Cut the grapefruit in half and loosen the segments
    with a sharp spoon or a grapefruit knife. Either leave
    them in the skin or turn them out, with the juice, on
    to a small plate, dish or saucer.
2   Add a teaspoon of French dressing.
3   With scissors, snip over the top a little fresh mint *or*
    fresh parsley *or* small rings of just the green part (so
    often thrown away) of spring onion.

Sweet Grilled Grapefruit

Serves 1

INGREDIENTS

half a grapefruit   1–2 teaspoons golden syrup

METHOD

1   Loosen the segments of the grapefruit with a sharp
    knife.
2   Spoon on the golden syrup, keeping it towards the
    centre of the fruit so that it will not drip over the
    grill pan.
3   Place under the grill – near enough to the heat to
    warm but not too near so that it burns. Heat gently
    for about 5 minutes, until just warmed through.

Lamb Chops with Mint

Serves 2 (or any number, according to number of chops used)

INGREDIENTS

2 home-produced, tender lamb chops (preferably chump chops)
seasoned flour
one and a half oz. butter
grated rind of half a lemon

2–3 tablespoons lemon juice
1 level dessertspoon caster sugar
1 dessertspoon freshly chopped mint leaves
3 tablespoons water

METHOD

1 Dip the chops in the seasoned flour (see Glossary). Shake off excess flour.

2 Melt the butter and fry chops gently for about 15–20 minutes, or until cooked through, turning once or twice. (To test whether done, prick with a sharp pointed knife or skewer – the juice should be only slightly pink, and the flesh should not look raw.)

3 Remove chops and keep them warm.

4 Drain off the fat from the pan, leaving behind 1 dessertspoon of the pan juices. Add lemon rind, lemon juice, sugar, chopped mint and water; bring to the boil. Cook for 1 or 2 minutes then pour over the chops and serve.

Note. To chop mint easily, snip finely with sharp

scissors, or use a very sharp long knife on a chopping board, or invest in a small gadget which chops mint, parsley and other fresh herbs by the turning of a handle.

Comment from 'Meals for Pensioners' class, East Warwickshire College of Further Education, Rugby:
    'Fresh mint not always available but a good brand of dried mint was acceptable.'

Lamb Chop in a Marinade

When you grill lamb chops or cutlets quickly they tend to shrink, and it looks so mean to put a shrunken chop on the plate! So, keep them from shrinking with a marinade (see Glossary) of oil and orange juice made spicy with cinnamon, and leave them in the marinade for an hour or so before cooking.

Serves 2

INGREDIENTS

4 tablespoons oil
a little grated orange rind
2 tablespoons orange juice

one and a half teaspoons
    ground cinnamon
2–4 lamb chops or cutlets

METHOD

1   In a dish, stir together briskly the oil, orange rind, juice and cinnamon. This amount of cinnamon makes

the mixture go brown, but it gives a lovely flavour; you can use less if you wish.

2 Wash and dry the chops, then put them into this marinade and turn them occasionally. Leave them for an hour or so.

3 Grill the chops, basting them with the liquor. It smells and tastes savoury and they should be plump, not shrunken.

Lemon Yogurt

Serves 2 or 3 (keeps well, if cool and covered, for a second day)

INGREDIENTS

half a packet lemon jelly
1 small carton lemon yogurt*
2 teaspoons PLJ or other unsweetened Vitamin C lemon drink

  * If you cannot get lemon yogurt, you could substitute a mandarin yogurt.

METHOD

1 Make up the jelly with boiling water, using less water than recommended on the packet, so that the jelly will set well.

2 When cool but not yet set, stir in the yogurt and then the undiluted fruit drink.

3   If you like, pour into individual serving dishes. Leave
    to set.

If you prefer a light texture, more like a mousse, you
can whisk the mixture when it is on the point of setting,
then leave it a little longer to set.

Lester's Wonder Cake

According to Mr Lester – 'a creative kind of chef' (aged
seventy-nine when he sent me this recipe) – this is an
extravagant recipe only for special friends. It is very easy
to prepare and he recommends eating it during an
evening discussion or a game of cards . . .

Serves 10

Oven temperature: 350°F, gas mark 4

Cooking time: 30 minutes

INGREDIENTS

1 small packet of digestive
  biscuits (8 oz.)
3 cartons of sour cream

1 large can of fruit cocktail (1
  lb. 13 oz.)

You need a loose-bottom cake tin approximately 9 inches
in diameter.

METHOD

1   Crush the biscuits with a rolling pin until fine crumbs
    (this is easily done if the biscuits are put a few at a
    time into a paper or plastic bag).
2   Line the bottom of a *loose-bottom* cake tin with greased
    greaseproof paper, then add the crushed biscuits, and
    press down to a firm layer.
3   Drain off all the juice from the fruit salad, then mix
    the drained fruit with the sour cream and when well
    mixed pour the contents over the crushed biscuits.
4   Bake at 350°F, gas mark 4, for 30 minutes.
5   When cold, place the tin in the refrigerator until the
    cake is quite set. Do not attempt to turn it out, serve
    it from the base of the tin.

Using smaller quantities, I made six or seven little cakes
using paper cases:

INGREDIENTS

3 digestive biscuits   1 small can fruit cocktail
1 carton sour cream   (7 oz.)

METHOD

1   Crush the biscuits.
2   Stand the paper cases on a baking sheet. Press a layer
    of biscuit crumbs into each paper case (there is no
    need to grease the paper).
3   Mix the drained fruit with the sour cream and spoon

carefully on top of the crumbs, pressing gently with the spoon to level the top. If you like, you can decorate with a cherry from the canned fruit.

4 Bake at 350°F, gas mark 4, for 20 minutes.
5 When cold, they can be served in the case or gently lifted out.

Liver and Orange

Serves 2

INGREDIENTS

4 slices of liver (lamb or calf)
seasoning
1 orange
1 small onion or 2 shallots
a knob of butter or margarine

1 dessertspoon oil
3–4 fluid oz. cider or red wine
pinch of mixed herbs
chopped parsley (optional)

METHOD

1 Wash the liver and pat dry on kitchen paper. Season.
2 Cut the orange across in slices – if you like a slightly bitter flavour, the orange should be sliced unpeeled.
3 Chop the onion or shallots finely.
4 Heat the butter or margarine with the oil in a frying pan and fry the liver, orange and onion – the liver should be just cooked, the orange lightly browned and the onion transparent and golden.
5 Add the cider or wine, mixed herbs and a little seasoning to taste and simmer until the liquid is reduced.
6 Serve, sprinkled with chopped parsley if liked.

Mincemeat Plait

Serves 4–6

Oven temperature: 425°F, gas mark 7

Cooking time: 20–25 minutes

INGREDIENTS

1 small packet (about seven and a half oz.) frozen puff pastry

quarter of a lb. mincemeat
icing sugar

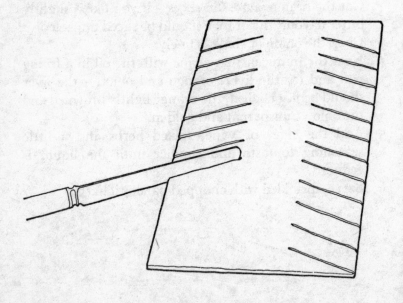

METHOD

1 Roll out puff pastry thinly into a rectangle (roughly 8 inches by 12 inches).

2 Mark the rectangle into three lengthwise. Trim the edges. On the two outside sections, cut pastry into 1-inch strips – slanting downwards.

3 Spread the mincemeat on the centre portion of the pastry.

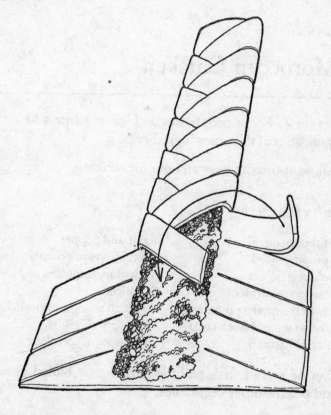

4 Dampen the edges of the pastry and fold the cut strips alternately over the mincemeat.
5 Press the two edges top and bottom and knock with the back of a knife to seal.
6 Bake on a baking sheet at 425°F, gas mark 7, for 20–25 minutes.
7 Cool and dredge with a little sieved icing sugar.

Moroccan Chicken

Serves 4. For 2 people use 2 chicken joints and smaller quantities of the sauce ingredients.

Allow approximately an hour for cooking.

INGREDIENTS

1 tablespoon oil
2 onions, sliced
4 chicken joints
1 teaspoon turmeric
one and a quarter pints stock, or water and stock cube
juice of 1 lemon

salt and pepper
1 tablespoon granulated sugar
1 lemon, unpeeled and thinly sliced
1 small orange, unpeeled and thinly sliced
2 teaspoons cornflour

Can be served with plain boiled rice or boiled potatoes and peas or other vegetables.

METHOD

1　Heat oil and fry onions without browning.
2　When transparent add chicken joints and fry slowly for 10 minutes.
3　Add turmeric and stir well; pour on the stock and lemon juice.
4　Bring to the boil and season to taste, then add the sugar.
5　Simmer slowly for 20–30 minutes. Add the sliced lemon and orange and simmer for a further 10 minutes.
6　Blend the cornflour with a little water and add to chicken dish; boil for a further 2 minutes.
7　Serve with plain boiled rice or boiled potatoes.

Oat Date Cookies

Makes 12 cookies

Oven temperature: 375°F, gas mark 5

Cooking time: 25–35 minutes

INGREDIENTS

8 oz. stoned cooking dates, chopped
quarter of a pint water
4 oz. porridge oats

4 oz. self-raising flour, sieved
4 oz. margarine
2 oz. soft brown sugar

METHOD

1   Grease a 7-inch square shallow tin.
2   Place the dates in a small saucepan with the quarter pint of water, bring to the boil and simmer for 5 minutes until the dates have absorbed most of the water.
3   Mix the oats with the flour and with the finger tips rub in margarine.
4   Stir in sugar.
5   Press half the dry mixture into the prepared tin. Lift out dates so that they are not too wet and spread them over the mixture. Cover with the remaining mixture and press down well.
6   Bake at 375°F, gas mark 5, for 25–35 minutes.
7   Mark into squares and remove from the tin when cold.

Peanut Butter Cookies

Are you ever asked to contribute to a local charity fête or fair? For such an occasion I have chosen this recipe because it makes plenty of biscuits with just 2 or 3 minutes' mixing time, no laborious rolling out, and only 7–10 minutes' baking for each batch. They are 'short' yet slightly chewy and have a mild peanut-butter flavour popular with adults as well as children.

Makes about 5 dozen biscuits

Oven temperature: 375°F, gas mark 5

Cooking time: 7–10 minutes for each batch.

INGREDIENTS

4 oz. Flora or other soft margarine
3 level tablespoons peanut butter
3 oz. caster sugar
3 oz. soft brown sugar
1 egg, not too large
6 oz. plain flour
half a level teaspoon baking powder
three quarters of a level teaspoon bicarbonate
   of soda   } sieved together
quarter of a level teaspoon salt

METHOD

1   Place all ingredients in a mixing bowl and beat to-
    gether with a wooden spoon until well mixed (2–3
    minutes).
2   Gather the mixture together with the fingertips. Take
    small pieces of the mixture, and roll into a ball the
    size of a cherry.
3   Place on a greased baking tray fairly wide apart
    (because they spread during cooking). Flatten with
    the prongs of a floured fork.
4   Bake on the middle shelf of a preheated oven at 375°F,
    gas mark 5, for 7–10 minutes. Cool on a wire tray.

Pork and Vegetables

Serves 3 good helpings

Allow at least 1 hour 15 minutes for cooking

INGREDIENTS

1 lb. lean belly pork	2 carrots, peeled and cut large
half to 1 firm small white cabbage (about 1 lb.)	black pepper
	a few caraway seeds (optional)
2 onions, peeled and cut large	chicken or herb stock cube

METHOD

1 Bone the pork and cut the meat into finger-sized portions, trimming away excess fat if necessary.
2 Put into cold water, together with the bones, and bring to the boil. Skim, cover and simmer till half cooked (approximately 40 minutes). Remove the bones.
3 Add the cabbage (trimmed and cut into eighths) and the onions and carrots.
4 Season with pepper and sprinkle on a few caraway seeds to 'buck up' the flavour.
5 Cover and continue simmering until cooked (approximately 30 minutes).
6 Strain off the meat and vegetables and keep hot. Return the liquid to the pan and boil it hard to reduce it, adding chicken or herb stock cube to flavour it

well. Pour a little of the stock over the meat and
vegetables and serve hot. The rest of the stock can be
used for soup the next day.

Priory Biscuits

This is one of several excellent tested recipes sent to me
from Cassio College, Watford, which runs a class
'Cookery for Blind Students'.

Makes about 20

Oven temperature: 325–350°F, gas mark 3–4

Cooking time: about 8 minutes

INGREDIENTS

2 oz. margarine or butter
2 oz. caster sugar
2 oz. self-raising flour
pinch salt
quarter of a level teaspoon
    baking powder

2 oz. rolled oats
1 tablespoon golden syrup
one and a half teaspoons hot
    water

METHOD

1   Grease a baking tray.
2   Cream fat and sugar and stir in the sifted flour, salt
    and baking powder.

3 Mix in the oats, syrup and water.
4 Allow to stand for half an hour.
5 Place widely spaced teaspoonfuls on the baking sheet.
6 Cook until slightly golden at 325–350°F, gas mark
   3–4. This should take approximately 8 minutes.
7 Leave to cool before removing from the baking sheet.

Red Cabbage

Serves 2 – any left over can be reheated next day; the
flavour even improves with keeping

INGREDIENTS

half a small red cabbage   1 heaped dessertspoon
a knob of dripping   cornflour
1 tablespoon granulated sugar   1–2 tablespoons vinegar
water in which the cabbage
  boils

METHOD

1 Wash the cabbage and cut into shreds, discarding the
   very tough leaves and stalk. Cover with lightly salted
   water and boil for 10 minutes. Drain, keeping the
   cooking water.
2 Melt the dripping and stir in the sugar. Gradually
   and smoothly stir in some of the purple cooking water.

Blend in the cornflour (see Glossary) and stir till slightly thickened.

3 Stir in the vinegar and the cooked cabbage. (The cabbage will turn an attractive red-purple with the vinegar.) Simmer gently in the oven or on top of the stove for an hour or longer, stirring occasionally.

Notes from test cooking. At step 2, if it seems too thick, add a little more cooking water. Or, if it is too runny, mix a little more cornflour with cold water, add to the liquid and bring back to the boil.

At step 3, if you like it tart you can add a little more vinegar – tastes vary.

Red cabbage does not overcook if it simmers for several hours.

Sausages – Sweet and Sour

Serves 2

Allow at least 30 minutes total cooking time for pork sausages, maybe a little less for beef.

INGREDIENTS

half a lb. pork or beef sausages
1 onion, peeled and chopped

salt and pepper
a clove or bay leaf

Sauce

1 tablespoon cornflour	small can crushed pineapple
1 tablespoon brown sugar (or golden syrup)	1 teaspoon dry mustard
1 tablespoon vinegar	1 teaspoon Marmite or Worcestershire sauce

For a more substantial meal, serve with mashed potato, boiled rice or spaghetti.

METHOD

1   Prick the sausages well and cook slowly in a pan until brown.
2   Remove the sausages from the pan, but leave the fat which has come out of them.
3   Cook the chopped onion in the sausage fat until soft.
4   Mix all the sauce ingredients together, then stir into the onion in the pan.
5   Add salt, pepper and bay leaf or clove. Bring the sauce to the boil, stirring constantly.
6   Cut the sausages in pieces and heat through in the sauce, making sure they are thoroughly cooked.

Savoury Egg Custard

Sent by Miss K. Barnett of London, sw10.

Serves 2

Oven temperature: 350°F, gas mark 4

Cooking time: 30–35 minutes

INGREDIENTS

grated cheese	salt and pepper
2 eggs	2 tomatoes
quarter of a pint milk	a knob of butter

METHOD

1 Grease an ovenproof dish and cover fairly thickly with grated cheese.
2 Beat the eggs, add the milk and seasoning and beat again.
3 Pour over the cheese.
4 Bake in the oven at 350°F, gas mark 4, for about 20 minutes, until the surface is set and starting to brown.
5 Take out of the oven and decorate with tomato pieces dotted with butter. Return to the oven for about 10–15 minutes until the surface is golden brown.

Note from test cooking. We agreed that this gave excellent light results. It is just the thing for good neighbour cookery – an easily shared meal. But it can be adjusted for one person by using only 1 large egg, just under a quarter of a pint of milk and 1 tomato.

Six Meals off One Chicken

This recipe was sent to me by Mr W. B. Sutton of Daventry, Northamptonshire, who has two good neighbours who share the midday meal with him on two days. This recipe is their favourite, and is economical.

First day: 3 meals

Cooking time: 1 hour 15 minutes, or a little longer

INGREDIENTS

1 roasting chicken weighing about 3 lb.
fresh parsley
thyme
lemon
salt and pepper

vegetables, e.g. potatoes, carrots, parsnips
a little yeast extract (Marmite) and a level tablespoon cornflour (optional)

METHOD

1   Wash the chicken, stuff with parsley (the more parsley the better the flavour), thyme and thin yellow parings of lemon peel.

2   Season inside and out with a generous measure of salt and pepper.

3   Place in a large saucepan, in 2 inches of water. Squeeze the juice of the lemon over the bird and add the giblets and a little salt to the water for flavouring the gravy.

4   Cover the pan with a tight fitting lid and simmer on a low heat for about 1 hour 15 minutes. Vegetables (whole or cut in chunks) can be added during the last 20–30 minutes if the saucepan is large enough for the liquor to cover them; otherwise they can be boiled separately.

5   Remove the bird and vegetables, and (optional) add a little Marmite for extra flavouring and blend in cornflour to thicken. Serve with gravy, but save at least half a pint of the gravy (keep very cold, preferably in a refrigerator) for the next day. There is usually enough chicken on one side of the bird for three helpings.

Second day : 3 meals of curry

INGREDIENTS

1 medium onion, chopped
2 oz. margarine
1 level tablespoon curry powder
1 level tablespoon cornflour
half a pint, or more, gravy from previous meal
1 apple, cored and chopped

1 tablespoon sultanas or mixed dried fruit
cut-up cooked chicken from previous meal
1 dessertspoon tomato ketchup
1 dessertspoon chutney

Serve with: boiled rice and green peas (allow about 2 oz. raw rice per person).

METHOD

1 Fry onion in the margarine in a saucepan.
2 Add curry powder and cornflour and fry for a minute.
3 Add gravy from the previous meal – at least half a pint – and stir well.
4 Stir in the chopped apple and dried fruit, bring to the boil and simmer very slowly, stirring occasionally, for 5–10 minutes. You may need to add a little more water if it is too thick.
5 Add the cut-up cooked chicken* to the curry and simmer for a further 5 or 10 minutes. Give it extra flavour by mixing in the tomato ketchup and chutney.
6 Serve in the centre of a mound of cooked rice, with green peas around the edge for effect.

  *To make yet another meal from the same chicken, save a few cubes of chicken breast for savoury dumplings, pages 227–8.

Syrupy Apple Puddings

Serves 2

Steaming time: 45 minutes

You will need two small individual pudding basins – or
cups.

INGREDIENTS

4 tablespoons golden syrup
2 oz. self-raising flour
pinch of salt
1 oz. shredded suet

2 tablespoons water
1 medium cooking apple,
    peeled and cored
a few currants (optional)

Can be served with custard.

METHOD

1 Grease the basins or cups and pour 1 tablespoon
    syrup into each.
2 Mix the flour, salt, suet and water to make a firm
    dough. Divide the pastry into halves.
3 Pat out two thirds of each half so that you can thinly
    line each basin, pressing the pastry gently down on
    top of the syrup.
4 Add thinly sliced apple, currants if used, and the re-
    maining tablespoon of syrup to each basin.
5 Pat out the rest of the pastry to form lids. Moisten the
    edges and press on the pastry lids to seal well.
6 Cover with greased foil or tied on greaseproof paper.

7   Steam (see Glossary) for 45 minutes. Turn out and
    serve hot, with custard if liked.

Topside 'Ratatouille'

Serves 2 or more

Cooking time: at least 45 minutes

This makes a little expensive meat go a long way – and
you can use more vegetables if you like to make the meat
go even further.

INGREDIENTS

1 slice topside of beef (or
   grilling steak)
1–2 leeks
or
1–2 onions
2–3 tomatoes (fresh or canned)

2 oz. mushrooms
green pepper (optional)
butter and oil for frying
pepper and salt
chopped parsley (optional)

You need a thick frying pan which has a lid, or which can
be covered with a saucepan lid or with foil.

METHOD

1   Slice the topside or steak into thin slivers (or ask the
    butcher to do this for you).
2   Prepare and slice all the vegetables.

3   Melt a little butter in a thick frying pan, add a table-
    spoon of cooking oil, and when it is hot add the meat
    and vegetables and seasoning and stir around to fry
    without burning.
4   When it is beginning to soften, put the lid on the pan
    and simmer very gently till thoroughly cooked.
5   Taste for seasoning. Sprinkle with parsley and serve
    hot.

Woolton Pie

This was a war-time pie named after the famous Minister
of Food, Lord Woolton. It was first created and served at
Claridges to demonstrate a patriotic, meatless recipe. Mr
Parkinson – a former chef at Claridges – has sent me this
adapted recipe, scaled down for two servings. I showed it
to a former colleague, Joan Peters (we were both – very
young (!) – working at the Ministry of Food in the days
of food rationing). She sent me a copy of the original M.
of F. recipe leaflet, reminding me that when potatoes
were plentiful and cheap the pie was covered with a
potato pastry. If no fat could be spared, we recommended
instead a fatless wheatmeal pie crust (there was no white
flour in those stringent days).

It was – and still is – a delicious pie!

Serves 2

Oven temperature: 350–375°F, gas mark 4–5

Cooking time: after sweating the vegetables, up to 1 hour in oven to cook the pie

INGREDIENTS

a mixture of vegetables in season*

fat (margarine, lard or dripping)

salt and pepper

1 dessertspoon flour

piece of stock cube

Pastry

shortcrust, made with 4 oz. flour, 2 oz. fat, rubbed together, and a little water to mix to a firm pastry dough (see page 143)

*e.g. a little white heart of cabbage, a few pieces of cauliflower, a couple of sticks of celery, and one each of leek, onion, potato, carrot, turnip, if available.

METHOD

1 Wash and prepare the vegetables and cut them up roughly.

2 Heat a little fat in a saucepan, add the vegetables, season with salt and pepper, and cook, turning them over occasionally, until they are a light golden colour.

3 Add a dessertspoon of flour, and stir for a few minutes until the flour is cooked.

4   Transfer to a pie dish. Add a little water in which you have dissolved a piece of Oxo cube or chicken-stock cube or some yeast extract.

5   Cover with rolled out shortcrust pastry (see illustra-
    tions) and put in the oven to cook and brown, about
    1 hour.

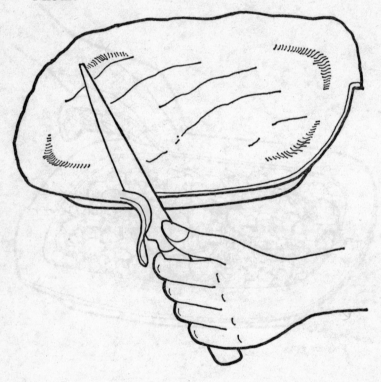

Chapter 5
Cookery from Your Store-cupboard

This is an extension of the 'Store-cupboard' chapter in
Easy Cooking for One or Two. The chapter roused a great
deal of interest not only from the housebound and those
looking after them, but also from men and women who
found that items from our shopping check list helped
them to remain independent.*

As we said before, you may be kept indoors by bad
weather or a temporary illness; the neighbour or home-
help who normally does your food buying may suddenly
have to cancel a visit, but with a stock of food in the home
there is no need to worry about immediate shopping.
Many of the canned, packaged and frozen foods are so

*A lecture kit based on this idea has been produced by the Geriatric
Nutrition Unit, Queen Elizabeth College, Campden Hill, London W8 7AH.
It is suitable for showing to groups and it includes lecture notes, coloured
cartoon slides and the check list in leaflet form for the audience. For further
details write (enclosing stamped addressed envelope) to Dr Louise Davies,
at the Geriatric Nutrition Unit (individual leaflets cannot be sent without
the full lecture kit).

easy to cook, or just turn out, that you need no guidance from me. The recipes in this chapter have been chosen to show you how you can 'dress up' some of the items to make a change.

There are other useful recipes for you in other chapters. Even if you cannot get to the shops you will probably have everything to hand for:

Cheese Spread

Sent by Mr W. B. Sutton.

Use a mature Cheddar if you like a strong flavour, medium Cheddar or Cheshire if you prefer a mild-flavoured spread.

INGREDIENTS

2 oz. grated cheese (Cheddar or Cheshire)	good dash of Worcestershire sauce
1 oz. plain flour	knob of butter
pepper and salt to taste	1 egg
3 or 4 tablespoons milk	

METHOD

1 Place all the ingredients, except the egg, in a saucepan and stir thoroughly.
2 Cook over a slow heat until the mixture has creamed (the cheese should be on the point of melting but it must not be overcooked). Remove from the heat.
3 Add the egg and beat in thoroughly.
4 Return to the heat, stirring. When it it has thickened (DO NOT BOIL) taste for seasoning, then empty into a greased receptacle.

Note. Cheese spread can be eaten hot or cold. For a snack meal spread it thickly on toast and brown it under the grill. It is good, cold, spread thickly on cracker biscuits. It will keep in a refrigerator or cold place for a few days, so it is a good stand-by to make for a day when you know you will not be going out shopping.

Chelsea Puddings

Serves 2 – for 1 make half quantity in one small individual basin (or an old china cup)

Steaming time: 45 minutes

INGREDIENTS

1 oz. self-raising flour
pinch of salt
1 oz. stale bread, crumbled
1 oz. shredded suet

1 oz. currants
1 oz. raisins
2 *level* teaspoons black treacle
2 teaspoons milk

Can be served with custard.

METHOD

1 Grease the basins or cups.
2 In a bowl, mix together the dry ingredients. With a wooden spoon, firmly beat in the treacle and milk.
3 Pack the mixture into the basins or cups – they should not be completely filled, leave a space for the puddings to rise.
4 Cover with greased foil or tie on some greaseproof paper.

5 Steam (see Glossary) for 45 minutes.
6 Turn out carefully and serve hot, with custard if liked.

Note from test cooking. These puddings only take a few moments to prepare – you don't even need to grate the bread, just pull it into small pieces.

It is easier to press on foil to cover than to make a secure lid of greaseproof paper. Alternatively, nowadays you can buy individual, boilable, plastic pudding basins which have plastic lids.

Frankfurter Bake

A *Yours* prizewinner which we have adapted so that it can be made from items in the store-cupboard. Sent by Miss K. Barnett of London, sw10.

Serves 2

Oven temperature: 300°F, gas mark 2

Cooking time: about 2 hours

INGREDIENTS

4 canned frankfurters (or use about 8 canned cocktail sausages)
2 eggs

quarter of a pint milk
salt and pepper
a little grated cheese (optional)

METHOD

1   Grease a fireproof dish and lay the sausages in it.
2   Beat the eggs into the milk and seasoning.
3   Pour over the sausages.
4   Grated cheese sprinkled over the top makes it more tasty.
5   Bake in the oven at 300°F, gas mark 2, for about 2 hours. The top should be golden brown with pieces of sausage peeping through.

Notes from test cooking. We tried this also with chipolata sausages (which were pricked once or twice with a fork to stop their skins bursting) and with skinless pork sausages. All were equally good, so choose the price and flavour which suits you best. Chipolatas and skinless pork sausages need to be used soon after purchase – they may keep about 3 days in a refrigerator.

French Salad Dressing

It saves time and washing up to keep a small quantity of French salad dressing (or *sauce vinaigrette*) in a screw top jar, ready to be shaken up and poured over a salad. Then you need not make it fresh each time. It keeps for about a week in a cool place.

INGREDIENTS

6 tablespoons corn oil
2 tablespoons vinegar
pinch of dry English mustard

shake of pepper
salt and sugar to taste

METHOD

1   Pour all the ingredients into a screw top jar, e.g. an empty clean salad-cream bottle, and shake vigorously to blend.
2   Taste a drop for flavour – I generally use about a quarter of a level teaspoon of salt and a little more of sugar.
3   Shake again before pouring a little over a salad just before serving.

JELLY DESSERTS

These are economical desserts – each uses only half a packet of jelly. Make up according to packet instructions, but use *a little less* water than recommended. If you are using evaporated milk, the remaining milk from the can may be served with the jelly, or with canned fruit, or in beverages requiring milk. Recipes sent by a *Yours* reader.

Chocolate Jelly

Serves 2 good helpings

INGREDIENTS

1 dessertspoon cocoa
a little sugar (1 teaspoon or
  less)
2 dessertspoons evaporated
  milk

half a packet jelly (e.g. lemon
  jelly)

METHOD

1 Mix the cocoa, sugar and evaporated milk to a *smooth*
   paste – do this carefully to avoid powdery or lumpy
   cocoa in the finished dish.
2 Add the half jelly, dissolved as directed but using a
   little less water than recommended on the packet.
   Mix well and leave in the cool to set.

Egg or Milk Jelly

Serves 2 good helpings

INGREDIENTS

half a packet jelly
1 tablespoon evaporated milk *or* 1 egg, beaten

METHOD

1   Dissolve the jelly as directed on the packet, but using a little less water.
2   When the jelly is cool but not yet set, beat in the evaporated milk *or* beat in the beaten egg. Leave to set.

Apple Jelly

Serves 2 good helpings

INGREDIENTS

1 large cooking apple
about half a pint water*

half a packet of jelly
about 1 tablespoon sugar

   * You will need a little *less* water than is called for to make up the half packet of jelly.

METHOD

1   Peel, core and roughly slice the apple.
2   Stew with the measured water until the apple is soft.
3   Drain off the hot liquor onto the jelly cubes and stir to melt the jelly.
4   Mash or sieve the apple, sweetening to taste, and stir into the jelly.
5   Leave to set.

Lemon Mousse

Serves 4 (enough for 2 on one day; keep in the cold for a second helping next day)

INGREDIENTS

half a lemon jelly
1 egg, separated
1 small can unsweetened evaporated milk
   (look for label saying extra vitamin D has been added)

METHOD

1   Dissolve jelly cubes in a quarter of a pint of boiling water. Cool.
2   Add egg yolk and beat.
3   Beat together the evaporated milk and egg white until foaming with air. Add to the jelly and egg yolk.
4   Stir occasionally until beginning to set.
5   Pour into serving dish or individual dishes.

Malt Bread

Makes a 1-lb. loaf.

A quick nourishing recipe which requires no kneading. The mixture is made a little wetter than is normal for a loaf and is then beaten for a few minutes with the mixing spoon – that takes the place of kneading. But allow time for the mixture to rise before baking – it could take an hour or longer, depending on the temperature.

Oven temperature: 425°F, gas mark 7, reduced to 375°F, gas mark 5

Cooking time: 45 minutes, i.e. 15 minutes at the high temperature, then another 30 minutes at the lower temperature

INGREDIENTS

1 tablespoon black treacle
1 tablespoon extract of malt*
1 oz. butter or margarine
half an oz. fresh yeast
or
one and a half teaspoons dried yeast plus half a teaspoon sugar

6 fluid oz. (just over a quarter of a pint) tepid water
half a lb. plain flour
quarter of a level teaspoon salt
1 oz. sultanas

*Extract of malt is obtainable from some health-food shops and chemists.

You will need a 1-lb. loaf tin, well greased, and a plastic bag lightly oiled on the inside, *or* a clean tea towel.

METHOD

1 In a small saucepan, warm the treacle, malt and fat.
2 Cream the yeast with a little of the water. Add the rest of the water. If using dried yeast and sugar, leave to stand for 10 minutes.

3   Sift the flour and salt into a bowl and stir in the sultanas.

4   Add the yeast and treacle mixtures to the dry ingredients to make a batter and beat vigorously for a few minutes.

5   Turn into the well-greased 1-lb. loaf tin, cover with a clean cloth or slip into the oiled plastic bag, and put in a fairly warm place to rise to about double its bulk (be careful it does not stick to the cloth or plastic; if it does, scrape it off with a knife, but this is messy).

6   Bake at 425°F, gas mark 7, for 15 minutes. Reduce the heat to 375°F, gas mark 5, and continue to bake till browned and firm to the touch (approximately another 30 minutes).

7   Cool slightly, then turn out of the tin. Eat buttered when cold but fresh. If you don't want to use it for a day or two, it keeps best inside a plastic bag, loosely closed.

Notes from College of Further Education, Stafford. Three of the elderly students who tried this would have liked it sweeter, but it was generally thought to be an economical loaf. Some students made the mixture too wet or used too much treacle or malt (they found it difficult to measure – it needs to be scraped from the underside of the spoon so that only 1 level spoonful is used), but the lecturer had excellent results and no problems and found it very acceptable five days later.

One-stage Cheese Loaf

Oven temperature: 375°F, gas mark 5

Cooking time: 40–45 minutes

You will need a 1-lb. loaf tin.

INGREDIENTS

8 oz. self-raising flour
1 level teaspoon baking powder
1 level teaspoon dry mustard } sieved together
half a level teaspoon salt
good shake of pepper
3 oz. soft margarine
1 egg, standard
3 oz. grated Cheddar cheese
8 tablespoons milk (a quarter of a pint)

METHOD

1 Grease and line the bottom of a 1-lb. loaf tin (or use a non-stick loaf tin). See Glossary.
2 Place all the ingredients in a mixing bowl and beat together with a wooden spoon for a couple of minutes until well mixed.
3 Spoon mixture into prepared tin and smooth the top.
4 Bake in a preheated oven at 375°F, gas mark 5, for 40–45 minutes.
5 Remove from the oven and leave to cool in tin for 5 minutes before turning out.

6   When cold serve slices spread with margarine or
    butter.

Note. This cheese loaf keeps well for several days in a
plastic bag.

Comment from 'Cookery for the Blind' class, Haywards Heath Adult Education Centre, Sussex: 'Students
were pleased with length of storage time. They also enjoyed slices toasted.'

Orange Juice Jelly

High in vitamin C.

INGREDIENTS

18 oz. (less than 1 pint)   half an oz. gelatine
   orange juice*   1 dessert apple (optional)

*e.g. from a carton, specifying vitamin C content, or from a
can, or reconstituted frozen, or fresh-squeezed juice. Do not use
an orange drink which does not contain vitamin C.

METHOD

1   In a small pan, gently warm about a quarter of a pint
    of the juice with the powdered gelatine to dissolve the
    gelatine – but do not let the liquid boil.
2   Stir in the rest of the juice. This cools the mixture
    down and avoids undue loss of vitamin C.

3   If liked, a peeled, cored dessert apple can be grated or
    finely chopped into the jelly before it is put to set. Or
    set some of the jelly plain and the rest (to be eaten on
    the day of making) with apple.
4   Put to cool and set.

Osborne Pudding

One of the recipes suggested by the students from Queen
Margaret College.

Serves 2 large helpings, or 4 small (serve hot, but any left
over can be eaten cold later)

Oven temperature: 325–350°F, gas mark 3–4

Cooking time: 30 minutes (after preliminary time of 20
minutes)

INGREDIENTS

4 large slices brown or white   2 tablespoons marmalade
    bread   1 egg
or   1 oz. (2 level tablespoons)
6 slices from a small loaf   sugar
butter or margarine   half a pint milk

METHOD

1   Spread the bread with butter or margarine. Remove
    crusts.

2 Then spread 2 large, or 3 small, slices with marmalade.
3 Well grease a pie dish with butter or margarine and
   put in the bread and marmalade, cut up if necessary
   to fit in.
4 In a jug or basin beat the egg thoroughly with a fork,
   then beat in the sugar and milk.
5 Pour the milk mixture over the bread and marmalade
   and leave for 20 minutes.
6 Place the last 2 or 3 slices of bread and butter on
   top, butter side up.
7 Bake for 30 minutes at 325–350°F, gas mark 3–4.

Ovaltine Fruit Loaf

Oven temperature: 325°F, gas mark 3

Cooking time: 1 hour

INGREDIENTS

4 oz. (one and a half small
   teacups) self-raising flour
one and a half oz. (less than
   half a small teacup) caster
   sugar
2 oz. (half a small teacup)
   mixed dried fruit

half an oz. (2 tablespoons)
   Ovaltine
approximately quarter of a
   pint milk

You need a 1-lb. loaf tin or small cake tin, greased and
lined (see Glossary).

METHOD

1   Place the flour, sugar, fruit and Ovaltine in a bowl.
2   Stir in sufficient milk to make a stiff batter.
3   Turn into the prepared tin and bake at 325°F, gas mark 3, for 1 hour.
4   When baked, turn out and cool on a cake rack.
5   Use after keeping one day (preferably loosely wrapped in a plastic bag or foil). Cut in thin slices and spread with margarine.

Peas and Batter

Serves 2

INGREDIENTS

2 small cups milk
knob of butter
salt

small packet frozen peas
a little fresh mint (optional)

Batter

1 oz. plain flour
pinch of salt
1 standard egg

2 tablespoons milk
1 tablespoon water

METHOD

1   Make the batter in the usual way (this is described in step-by-step method on pp. 90–91, Bacon and Kidney Toad-in-the-Hole).

2 In a medium-sized saucepan bring the 2 small cups of milk to the boil with the butter and a little salt.

3 Simmer the peas in the milk for a couple of minutes. Snip some fresh mint into the milk if the peas are not the 'minted' variety.

4 Spoon the batter into the boiling milk, using a dessertspoon. It will look thin and runny but during about 4 minutes' boiling (watch so that it does not boil over) you will find it sets into a light mixture which can be lifted and turned with the spoon.

5 Serve in a soup plate for a comforting, warm soup-cum-snack.

Prunes and Grapefruit

This is a refreshing start to breakfast – or a quick dessert. It is especially nourishing because the vitamin C in the grapefruit probably helps the body to absorb the iron in the prunes.

INGREDIENTS

canned grapefruit segments   canned prunes

METHOD

1 Mix the two fruits together, with some of their juice, in a cereal bowl.

2 Turn any unused fruits out of the cans into a bowl.
   Cover and keep cool till used later that day or the
   next.

Raisin Shortbread

Oven temperature: 325°F, gas mark 3

Cooking time: 45–50 minutes

INGREDIENTS

4 tablespoons orange juice or   6 oz. plain flour
   orange squash   2 oz. caster sugar
3–4 oz. seedless raisins   4 oz. butter

METHOD

1 In a small saucepan bring orange juice and seedless
   raisins slowly to the boil. Turn into a basin and leave
   to cool.
2 Sieve flour into a mixing bowl, add sugar and rub in
   butter until the mixture resembles breadcrumbs.
3 Knead *half* the crumble mixture to form a dough.
4 Press the dough into a shallow baking tin 7–8 inches
   in diameter (the kind used for Victoria sandwich
   cakes).
5 Spoon raisins over dough, leaving behind any surplus
   orange juice.

6   Sprinkle the other half of the crumble mixture all
    over the top of the raisins and gently but firmly press
    into a dough with the palm of the hand.
7   Bake at 325°F, gas mark 3, until beginning to turn a
    pale biscuit colour, approximately 45–50 minutes.
8   Mark into eight to ten segments and, when cool,
    remove from the tin.

Refrigerator Cheese Biscuits

Makes approximately 25 small biscuits to serve with a
mid morning or evening drink. The mixture can be left
raw for several days in the cabinet of the refrigerator, or
kept till needed in a freezer, so this is an ideal mixture to
be prepared in advance and cooked at the last minute for
unexpected guests.

Oven temperature: 400°F, gas mark 6

Cooking time: 7–10 minutes

INGREDIENTS

2 oz. medium or strong   1 oz. margarine
   Cheddar cheese, finely   a few drops Worcestershire
   grated   sauce
1 oz. self-raising flour   salt and pepper

METHOD

1   Mix all ingredients together (if using hard margarine, allow to soften at room temperature). If you are using a mixing machine the dough is made in a few moments.
2   Using a little flour on the board, roll with the hands into a long sausage, approximately the diameter of a 10p piece.
3   Wrap loosely in foil and put in the refrigerator to harden for several hours or longer.
4   With a sharp knife, cut into thin slices, not more than a quarter of an inch thick. Place on baking sheet.
5   Bake at 400°F, gas mark 6, until just beginning to turn golden round the edges (approximately 7–10 minutes).

Note. You can bake a few biscuits at a time and put the rest of the raw mixture back in the refrigerator until needed.

Russian Cream

Sent by Mrs Henrietta Kitchiner, Bexleyheath – a *Yours* prizewinner.

Serves 2 large or 4 small portions; keeps well in the cold (preferably a refrigerator) from one day to the next.

INGREDIENTS

1 egg, separated   a few drops of vanilla essence
half a pint milk   about 2 teaspoons drinking
quarter of a cup sugar (two to   chocolate (optional)
   two and a half tablespoons)
half a packet gelatine (one and
   a half teaspoons)

METHOD

1 Roughly mix the egg yolk and stir into the milk in a
   saucepan, along with the sugar, gelatine and vanilla
   essence.
2 Bring just up to the boil, stirring to dissolve the sugar
   and gelatine, but do not boil. If you like a chocolate
   flavour, stir in briskly the drinking chocolate (amount
   according to taste).
3 Whisk white of egg till stiff (to save washing up this
   can be done in the dish in which it is to be served).
4 Pour the hot milk mixture straight over the egg
   whites, stirring gently with a fork to mix. Allow to
   set.

Comment from 'Meals for Pensioners' class, East Warwickshire College of Further Education, Rugby:
   'Fifteen of our students tried this recipe; all liked it very
much. All fifteen said they will prepare it for themselves at
home, even though most of them do not generally use
gelatine.'

Hot Sardine and Tomato

Serves 2

This is an easy way to serve sardines hot.

Oven temperature: 400°F, gas mark 6 (OR use the grill, medium heat)

Cooking time: 8 minutes to cook tomato sauce, 10 minutes to bake in oven, or less if using grill

INGREDIENTS

small can of sardines
oil from the sardine can
2 large tomatoes (or equivalent canned, peeled tomatoes)
clove of garlic (optional)

or

1 small onion, sliced
salt and pepper
1 tablespoon dry breadcrumbs (optional)

METHOD

1 Drain the sardines, reserving the oil in the can and arrange the fish in a lightly greased baking dish.
2 Peel the tomatoes if necessary. Crush the garlic or slice the onion finely.
3 Combine chopped-up tomatoes, garlic or onion, and oil in a small saucepan, sprinkle with salt and pepper and cook over low heat for 8 minutes.
4 Pour over the sardines. If you are using breadcrumbs,

sprinkle them over the top, moistening them with a little oil.

5   *Either* brown in oven at 400°F, gas mark 6, for 10 minutes. *Or*, if the oven is not being used, brown in a few minutes under a medium grill.

Spicy Rice Pudding

Serves 3 – some can be eaten cold with stewed fruit next day

Oven temperature: 300°F, gas mark 2

Cooking time: 2 hours to 2 hours 15 minutes

INGREDIENTS

one and a half oz. short-grain
   rice
half to one oz. sugar
1 level teaspoon ground
   cinnamon *or* mixed spice

1 pint milk
a knob of butter or margarine

METHOD

1   Wash the rice through a sieve and place it in a greased ovenproof dish with the sugar, spice (either cinnamon or mixed spice) and milk. Stir well.

2   Dot the top with shavings of butter or margarine.

3   Cook in a slow oven, 300°F, gas mark 2, for 2 hours to

2 hours 15 minutes, stirring once or twice in the first hour or so. When ready, the rice should be tender and the milk nearly absorbed.

4 If some is left to get cold for eating next day, it is advisable to serve with stewed fruit to liven up the colour.

To cook on top of the stove

This is only recommended if you can control the heat to maintain a *very gentle* simmer, otherwise there is a danger of the milk boiling over.

Cooking time: 1 hour to 1 hour 30 minutes

INGREDIENTS

as above

METHOD

1 Put the washed rice with the sugar, spice, milk and butter or margarine in a thick saucepan. Stir well.
2 Bring to the boil, stir, cover the pan with a lid and simmer *very gently* for 1 hour to 1 hour 30 minutes, stirring from time to time to avoid burning.

Store-cupboard Fish Cakes

This is adapted from a recipe for Tuna Fish Cakes, sent by Mrs D. Bull of Guildford, Surrey.

Since her recipe became a prizewinner in the *Yours* newspaper competition, the price of canned tuna has risen considerably but, so far, the price of canned mackerel remains low. The recipe can also be used with pilchards or any other favourite canned oily fish.

Serves 2

INGREDIENTS

small packet of instant mashed potato (preferably with added vitamin C noted on the packet)

small can mackerel or tuna
salt and pepper, if necessary
flour
lard or cooking oil

METHOD

1 Reconstitute the potato as directed on the packet, *but use a little less water* so that the mixture is fairly stiff. You may find that, if your appetite is small, you will want to use only half the packet, reserving the rest for another meal next day.

2 Mash in the mackerel. Do not add too much of the oil or the fish cakes will be too soft to handle.

3 Taste, and add seasoning if you think it necessary.

4 Turn onto a floured board. Divide and form into two large or four small fish cakes.

5   Fry in lard or cooking oil till well heated through and brown and crisp on the outside – turn them once or twice during cooking.

Notes from test cooking. Because this is a recipe from the store-cupboard, it recommends packet potato. But you could substitute a cupful of fresh or left-over mashed potato.

When we used a 7-oz. can of mackerel and a medium-sized packet of potato we made plenty for three people. But you could use less, and mash up the extra fish for a tasty sandwich filling. (Left-over fish should be turned out of the can and kept, covered, in a cool place overnight.)

Surprise Dumplings

Serves 2

Cooking time: 8–10 minutes

INGREDIENTS

2 oz. self-raising flour
pinch of salt

1 oz. shredded suet
water to mix

For savoury dumplings

Add a little grated lemon rind and a quarter of a teaspoon of

dried thyme to the dry ingredients; alternatively, just add half a
level teaspoon of dried herbs.

Fillings

Savoury: small pieces of cooked liver, kidney, chicken, beef,
pork, lamb, bacon; or pickled onions or canned mushrooms.

Sweet: small pieces of apple or pear, pineapple chunks, glacé
or stoned canned cherries.

METHOD

1 Mix together the flour, salt and suet with sufficient
water to make a firm dough. Knead lightly.
2 Divide the dough into four pieces and flatten with the
hand.
3 Place a piece of filling in the centre of each round of
dough and enclose. Pinch well together to make a
good seal and roll into balls. Dust with flour.
4 Place the dumplings in boiling salted water (or
stock/soup for savoury dumplings), cover and
simmer gently until the dumplings are cooked and
fluffy (about 8–10 minutes).
5 Remove with a draining spoon and serve immediately.

Serving suggestions: gravy and vegetables with savoury
dumplings; custard with sweet dumplings.

Teaspoon Biscuits

Makes approximately 15. When cold, store in a tin.

Oven temperature: 375°F, gas mark 5

Cooking time: approximately 15 minutes

INGREDIENTS

4 oz. margarine	quarter of a teaspoon vanilla
2 oz. caster sugar	essence
either	4 oz. plain flour
2 oz. glacé cherries	
or	
2 oz. plain chocolate	

METHOD

1 Cream margarine and sugar together until light and fluffy.
2 Chop the glacé cherries; *or* either cut or break the chocolate into small pieces.
3 Stir in cherries *or* chocolate, vanilla essence and flour to form a soft dough.
4 Place teaspoons of the mixture well apart on a greased baking sheet – they flatten and spread.
5 Bake at 375°F, gas mark 5, for about 15 minutes until beginning to turn pale golden.
6 Remove from the oven, leave on the baking sheet for a few minutes, then cool on a wire tray.

Vitamin C Drink

Serves 1

INGREDIENTS

PLJ or similar bottled lemon drink, unsweetened
Ribena or other vitamin C blackcurrant drink

METHOD

Pour a mixture of the lemon and blackcurrant drinks into a glass and fill up with hot water (for winter) or cold water (for a refreshing summer drink). The amounts and proportions depend on personal taste, so experiment to find the flavour most acceptable.

Note. I have specified a bottled vitamin C lemon drink because this is a 'store-cupboard' recipe. But if you have a fresh lemon in the house you can use the juice from this instead.

Welsh Rarebit with Egg

Sent by Miss Mary Flint, Nottingham.

Serves 1

INGREDIENTS

2 oz. Cheddar cheese, grated
  or Cheshire cheese,
  crumbled
one and a half tablespoons
  milk

knob of margarine or butter
shake of pepper
dash of Worcestershire sauce
1 egg, beaten
1 large slice of toast

METHOD

1 Slowly melt the cheese in a small saucepan with the milk, margarine, pepper and Worcestershire sauce, stirring all the time.

2 When melted, add the well beaten egg and continue to cook, stirring, for 2–3 minutes. Serve on toast.

Note from test cooking. If you find it troublesome to grate cheese, just cut Cheshire cheese into slices and then crumble them with the fingers.

CHOOSING THE FOODS FOR YOUR STORE-CUPBOARD

Do you read the labels on the foods you buy for your store-cupboard? They can be an eye-opener and I don't mean just because of their small print!

Do you realize that by law the ingredients are itemized 'in descending order of the proportion by weight in which they were used in the manufacturing process'? In other words, the ingredient mentioned first is the one in greatest quantity.

But do not expect to learn everything from the label. *Quality* is not shown. For that you must trust your own taste and preference.

If you are reading the contents of a packet containing dried ingredients, remember it is the very light *dried* weights which are listed in descending order. Once you have added water, the reconstituted weights might give a better picture. Still, read the long, long list of ingredients, e.g. on an 'instant' soup mix. Does it entice you? I get the feeling that a simple spoonful of yeast extract stirred into a cup of boiling water or milk could give more nourishment for my money!

In choosing foods for your store-cupboard (the same advice applies to someone else doing the shopping or cooking for you):

● Read the labels.
● Search for the smaller sizes if you think you would waste a bigger size.

- Look (with dismay!) at the price – shop around if you can. Nowadays prices, even of proprietary brands, vary widely from shop to shop.
- Make a list of the foods you enjoy – and 'black-list' any you find poor value for money.
- Follow the cooking instructions.

Glossary of Cooking Terms

I have had some delightful letters from readers of *Easy Cooking for One or Two*, who put their own interpretation on instructions such as 'poach', 'sweat', 'rub in', 'fold', 'coat' and other cookery terms, and say would I please *explain* what I mean! To save lengthy explanations in the recipes, I have compiled the following list of cooking terms used in this book.

Blend: to mix. For example, cornflour is blended with water by first being stirred with a spoonful or so of cold water; then, when it is a smooth paste, more liquid is added to thin it.

Blended cornflour (or other thickening such as flour, potato flour, arrowroot) can be used to thicken a hot mixture, e.g. a gravy, in the following way:

1 Pour some of the hot mixture onto the thinly blended cornflour, stirring.
2 Pour this back into the rest of the hot mixture, stirring it all the time and heating it until it thickens. (If you just poured the cold blended cornflour into the hot gravy it could lump.)

Boil: to keep a liquid at a temperature high enough to make it bubble.

Cake: to test when cooked:

1   Push a metal skewer or the flat blade of a knife down
    into the centre of the cake. If the cake is not cooked
    enough, the skewer or knife will come out sticky with
    the mixture – it should come out almost clean.
2   When the cake is cooked, it generally feels firm to the
    touch, and begins to shrink away slightly from the
    sides of the tin.
    Note: for light cakes such as sponge cakes, step 2 is
    the only necessary test.

Coat: to cover
  To coat with egg and breadcrumbs:
1   Beat up the egg in a shallow dish.
2   Pour some crumbs or raspings onto kitchen paper.
3   Dip the food into the egg. At this stage you can use a
    pastry brush to paint the food all over with the egg.
4   Lift (with a slice, see page 236), let the surplus egg drip
    off, then put the food into the crumbs and use the
    paper to shake the crumbs to stick over the food. It is
    then ready for cooking.

Cream: to mix fat and sugar together by beating (with a
wooden spoon) using a circular motion against the side
of the mixing bowl. They gradually blend into a soft,
pale mixture. When you lift some up over the bowl and
tap it against the rim, the mixture should easily fall off
the spoon.

Dropping consistency: the texture of a cake or pudding
before it is turned into the tin or basin to cook. Lift up a

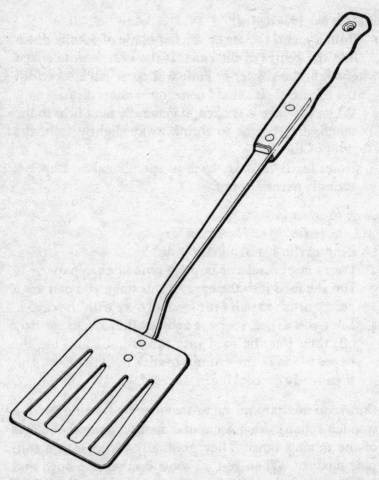

spoonful of the mixture and hold it steadily against the side of the mixing bowl. The lump should drop easily from the spoon within a few seconds.

Fold in (sometimes called 'to cut and fold'): to stir an

ingredient (such as flour or egg white) gently into a mixture so that it keeps its light or creamy texture. Typically, flour is folded into a sponge cake mixture; whisked egg whites are folded into a soufflé. Heavy

handling would crush out the air, so: use a thin metal spoon and cut the ingredient down into the mixture in a circular movement – down, round, up, down, round, up (see illustration) until the ingredient is mixed in quickly and smoothly. Not as difficult as it sounds.

Grease and line a tin: to rub the tin with margarine or lard (best to use a piece of greaseproof paper to handle the fat). If it is an awkward-shaped tin you may prefer to melt the fat and brush it on with a pastry brush.

If, in addition, the recipe calls for lining the tin, you still need to grease it lightly first so that the lining paper will stick smoothly. Then line the tin and brush the lining paper with melted fat.

To line: see illustration.

There is no need to grease and line if you have non-stick baking tins.

Marinade: a seasoned mixture of oil with vinegar, lemon (or orange) juice or wine, in which food is left for a given time. This helps to soften the fibres of meat or fish and adds flavour to the food.

Poach: to cook food, e.g. eggs, covered with simmering liquid. Use a shallow pan without a lid.

Roux: fat and flour stirred and cooked together to form the thickening basis for a sauce. The liquid is then added gradually. But in a one-stage sauce (see page 129) it is not necessary to go to the trouble of making a roux.

Rub in: to mix fat into flour in the preparation of short-crust pastry, plain cakes and biscuits. Sieve the flour into a bowl. Add the fat and cut it up into small pieces. Then rub it gently but firmly into the flour with the fingertips, lifting up the hands frequently so that air gets into the mixture. When rubbed in, the mixture resembles large breadcrumbs. (See illustrations pages 240–41).

Scald: to pour boiling water over the food (or, if you feel this is safer, to lower the food into a bowl of water that has

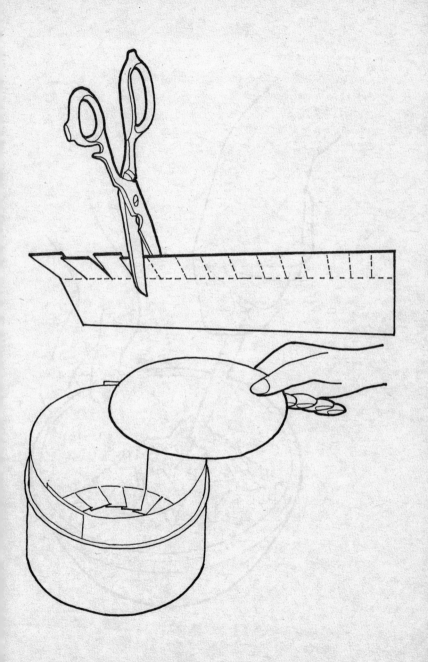

just boiled). Leave only for a minute or less, then cool it under cold water so that it is easy to handle. Scalding makes it easy to remove the skin from tomatoes, peaches, etc.

Seasoned flour: a couple of tablespoons of flour mixed with a teaspoon of salt and a good shake of pepper. Use for

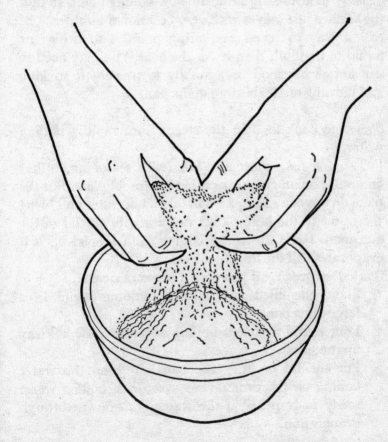

coating meat or fish before frying or stewing. Either dip the food into the seasoned flour and shake off excess, or – less messy – put the seasoned flour into a clean paper or plastic bag and shake the food in it so that it gets evenly coated.

Simmer : to keep a liquid just below boiling point, so that the surface just moves with very occasional bubbles. The easiest way to reach simmering point is to bring the liquid to the boil, then lower the heat. You may need to stir simmering food occasionally to prevent it sticking and burning on the bottom of the pan.

Steam : to cook food in the steam from rapidly boiling water.

To steam fish : Place the fish (with seasoning, butter and milk) on an enamel or other heatproof plate. Put the plate on top of a saucepan half full of hot water and bring the water to the boil. Cover the fish with the lid of the saucepan. Keep the water boiling (and topped up if it evaporates) till the fish is cooked.

To steam puddings if you do not possess a steamer:

1 Stand the filled and covered pudding basins in a large saucepan.
2 Pour round sufficient boiling water to come halfway up the sides.
3 Put the lid on the saucepan and keep the water boiling all the time. Have a kettle of boiling water ready to 'top up' if the water boils down through evaporation.

4   Lift the basins out carefully (I protect my hands with washing up gloves).

To steam vegetables: place the vegetables in a metal colander and put this over the pan of boiling water so that it dips into the pan but does not touch the water. Cover the vegetables with the saucepan lid.

Sweat: to cook vegetables very gently in melted fat till they begin to soften and exude juice.

Timing a meal: Inexperienced cooks often having difficulty in getting all the items for one meal ready for eating at the same time. You need to 'think backwards'. Look at the timings of the recipes. You may find that the meat course will take 1 hour 30 minutes, the greens will take 7 minutes, the potatoes 20 minutes and the hot dessert 45 minutes. Do not panic! If, say, you want to eat at about 12.45, see sample timetable below:

11.15   Put meat course on to cook.
12.00   Put dessert on to cook.
12.25   Put potatoes on to cook.
12.40   Put greens on to cook.
12.45   Start dishing up – the greens should be ready by the time you have dished up the meat and potatoes.

● Always allow plenty of time for preparing the recipe.
● But do not prepare vegetables long in advance, and do not cook them early then keep them warm; both practices would be death to vitamin C.

● You may prefer to start cooking the dessert 5 or 10
  minutes later so that it is just cooked by the time you
  finish the first course. But most desserts can be dished
  up and kept warm while you eat.

Weights and Measures

SOLID MEASURES

British   *Metric*

16 oz. = 1 lb.   1000 grammes (g) = 1 kilogramme (kilo)

Approximate equivalents

BRITISH	METRIC	METRIC	BRITISH
1 lb. (16 oz.)	450 g	1 kilo (1000 g)	2 lb. 3 oz.
½ lb. (8 oz.)	225 g	½ kilo (500 g)	1 lb. 2 oz.
¼ lb. (4 oz.)	100 g	¼ kilo (250 g)	9 oz.
1 oz.	25 g	100 g	4 oz.

LIQUID MEASURES

British

1 quart = 2 pints	= 40 fl. oz.
1 pint = 4 gills	= 20 fl. oz.
½ pint = 2 gills	
or 1 cup	= 10 fl. oz.
¼ pint = 8 tablespoons	= 5 fl. oz.
1 tablespoon	= just over ½ fl. oz.
1 dessertspoon	= ⅓ fl. oz.
1 teaspoon	= ⅙ fl. oz.

Metric

1 litre = 10 decilitres (dl) = 100 centilitres (cl) = 1000 millilitres (ml)

Approximate equivalents

BRITISH	METRIC	METRIC	BRITISH
1 quart	1.1 litres	1 litre	35 fl. oz.
1 pint	6 dl	$\frac{1}{2}$ litre (5 dl)	18 fl. oz.
$\frac{1}{2}$ pint	3 dl	$\frac{1}{4}$ litre (2.5 dl)	9 fl. oz.
$\frac{1}{4}$ pint (1 gill)	1.5 dl	1 dl	4 fl. oz.
1 tablespoon	15 ml		
1 dessertspoon	10 ml		
1 teaspoon	5 ml		

American

1 quart = 2 pints	= 32 fl. oz.
1 pint = 2 cups	= 16 fl. oz.
1 cup	= 8 fl. oz.
1 tablespoon =	$\frac{1}{2}$ fl. oz.
1 teaspoon =	$\frac{1}{6}$ fl. oz.

Approximate equivalents

BRITISH	AMERICAN	AMERICAN	BRITISH
1 quart	2$\frac{1}{2}$ pints	1 quart	1$\frac{1}{2}$ pints + 3 tbs
1 pint	1$\frac{1}{4}$ pints		(32 fl. oz.)
$\frac{1}{2}$ pint	10 fl. oz. (1$\frac{1}{4}$ cups)	1 pint	$\frac{3}{4}$ pint + 2 tbs
$\frac{1}{4}$ pint (1 gill)	5 fl. oz.		(16 fl. oz.)
1 tablespoon	1$\frac{1}{2}$ tablespoons	1 cup	$\frac{1}{2}$ pint − 2 tbs
1 dessertspoon	1 tablespoon		(8 fl. oz.)
1 teaspoon	$\frac{1}{3}$ fl. oz.		

HANDY MEASURES

breadcrumbs, fresh	1 oz. = 7 level tablespoons approximately
„ dried	1 oz. = 6 „ „ „
packet crumbs	1 oz. = 4 „ „ „
cheese, Cheddar, grated	1 oz. = 3 „ „ „
cocoa powder	1 oz. = 3 „ „ „

cornflour, custard powder	1 oz. = 2 level tablespoons approximately		
dried fruit (currants, sultanas, raisins)	1 oz. = 2 „	„	„
flour, unsifted	1 oz. = 3 „	„	„
rice, uncooked	1 oz. = 2 „	„	„
rolled oats	1 oz. = 4 „	„	„
semolina	1 oz. = 2 „	„	„
suet, packet shredded	1 oz. = 3 „	„	„
sugar, granulated, caster, demerara	1 oz. = 2 „	„	„
syrup, honey, treacle	1 oz. = 1 „	„	„

8 tablespoons liquid = 5 fluid oz. = quarter of a pint

Egg Sizes

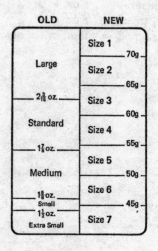

OLD	NEW
	Size 1
Large	70g
	Size 2
2⅜ oz.	65g
	Size 3
Standard	60g
	Size 4
1⅞ oz.	55g
	Size 5
Medium	50g
1⅝ oz.	Size 6
Small	45g
1½ oz.	Size 7
Extra Small	

Equivalent Oven Temperatures

Degrees Fahrenheit	Gas Mark	Degrees Centigrade	Heat of Oven
225°F	1/4	110°C	Very cool
250°F	1	130°C	Very cool
275°F	1	140°C	Cool
300°F	2	150°C	Cool
325°F	3	170°C	Moderate
350°F	4	180°C	Moderate
375°F	5	190°C	Fairly hot
400°F	6	200°C	Fairly hot
425°F	7	220°C	Hot
450°F	8	230°C	Very hot
475°F	9	240°C	Very hot

List of Illustrations

Index

Toast
  cinnamon, 13–14
  cream cheese, 14–15
  hot sardine, 32–3
Toasted sandwiches, 29
Today and tomorrow neck
    chops, 74–6
Tomato
  and basil salad, 148–9
  and hot sardine, 223–4
Topside 'ratatouille', 196–7
Tuna
  canned, fish cakes, 226–7
  in roll mop salad, 27
Turkey in mustard-cheese
    sauce, 101–2

Vegetables
  and pork, 186–7
  salad, canned, 27
  to steam, 243
  stew, 149–50
Vitamin C drink, 230

Welsh rarebit
  with egg, 231
  simple, 77
Wholemeal tart, 140–41
Woolton pie, 197–200

Yogurt, lemon, 175–6
Yours, ix, 39

FOR THE BEST IN PAPERBACKS, LOOK FOR THE 🐧

In every corner of the world, on every subject under the sun, Penguin represents quality and variety – the very best in publishing today.

For complete information about books available from Penguin – including Puffins, Penguin Classics and Arkana – and how to order them, write to us at the appropriate address below. Please note that for copyright reasons the selection of books varies from country to country.

In the United Kingdom: Please write to *Dept E.P., Penguin Books Ltd, Harmondsworth, Middlesex, UB7 0DA.*

If you have any difficulty in obtaining a title, please send your order with the correct money, plus ten per cent for postage and packaging, to *PO Box No 11, West Drayton, Middlesex*

In the United States: Please write to *Dept BA, Penguin, 299 Murray Hill Parkway, East Rutherford, New Jersey 07073*

In Canada: Please write to *Penguin Books Canada Ltd, 2801 John Street, Markham, Ontario L3R 1B4*

In Australia: Please write to the *Marketing Department, Penguin Books Australia Ltd, P.O. Box 257, Ringwood, Victoria 3134*

In New Zealand: Please write to the *Marketing Department, Penguin Books (NZ) Ltd, Private Bag, Takapuna, Auckland 9*

In India: Please write to *Penguin Overseas Ltd, 706 Eros Apartments, 56 Nehru Place, New Delhi, 110019*

In the Netherlands: Please write to *Penguin Books Netherlands B.V., Postbus 195, NL–1380AD Weesp*

In West Germany: Please write to *Penguin Books Ltd, Friedrichstrasse 10–12, D–6000 Frankfurt/Main 1*

In Spain: Please write to *Longman Penguin España, Calle San Nicolas 15, E–28013 Madrid*

In Italy: Please write to *Penguin Italia s.r.l., Via Como 4, I-20096 Pioltello (Milano)*

In France: Please write to *Penguin Books Ltd, 39 Rue de Montmorency, F-75003 Paris*

In Japan: Please write to *Longman Penguin Japan Co Ltd, Yamaguchi Building, 2-12-9 Kanda Jimbocho, Chiyoda-Ku, Tokyo 101*

Louise Davies in Penguin Books

EASY COOKING FOR ONE OR TWO

A new edition of the bestselling cookery book that has transformed eating for those who live alone or find cooking difficult and tiring.

Most cookery books cater for four or more. For smaller numbers you are often left to choose between wasteful, expensive dishes and a boring, unsound diet. Here Louise Davies solves the problem with over 150 delicious, easy and nutritious recipes in small quantities.

'This book is excellent, the recipes are cheap, easy to make even if you can't cook' – Sheila Hutchins in the *Daily Express*

'An excellent guide to maximum nutrition at minimum expense of both money and effort . . . I can't think of a better present to revive a flagging interest in cooking' – *Guardian*